BEYOND REASONABLE DOUBT

BLITZ EDITIONS

Published by Blitz Editions
an imprint of Bookmart Ltd
Registered Number 2372865
Trading as Bookmart Ltd
Desford Road
Enderby
Leicester LE9 5AD

ISBN 1 85605 258 3

This material has previously appeared in *Emergency Rescue*.

Every effort has been made to contact the copyright holders for the pictures. In some cases they have been untraceable, for which we offer our apologies.
Thanks to the following libraries and picture agencies:
Hulton-Deutsch Collection, Range/Bettman, Press Association, Associated Press, Solo Syndication, Joanna Nathan-Ayres.

This book was produced by Amazon Publishing Limited

Designed by Wilson Design Associates

Edited by Graham McColl

Printed in the Czech Republic
51779

BEYOND REASONABLE DOUBT

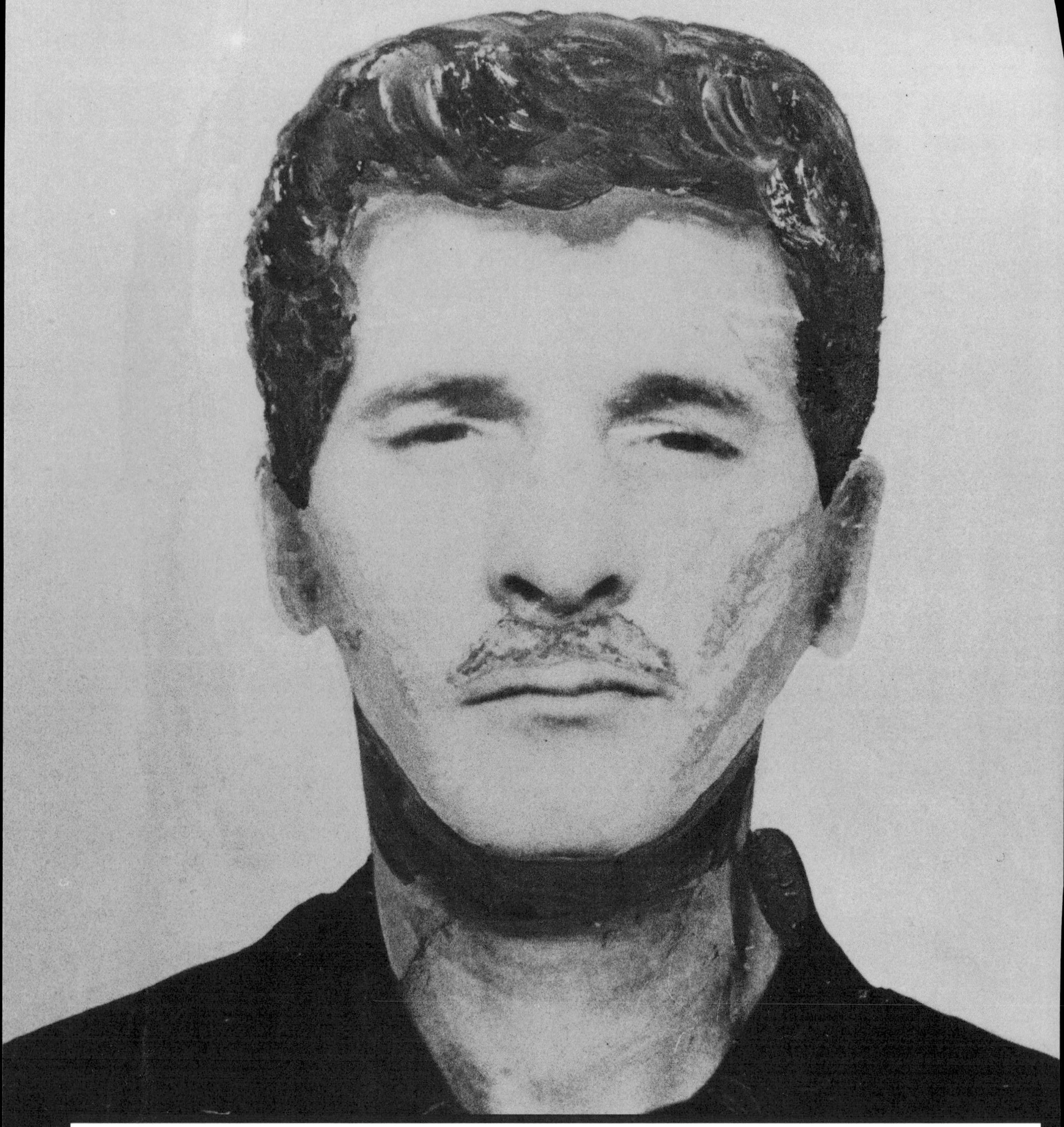

MURDER INC.
Cheapskate Killers

An innocuous block of flats in East London hid behind its walls scenes of medieval horror. There, the killing company known as Murder Inc. burned their victims in a tiny grate, later sprinkling their ashes from car windows. If ever criminals deserved to be found guilty, it was the perpetrators of these crimes.

He was one of the most formidable figures ever to stand in the dock of Number One Court at the Old Bailey; a small space that has seen some of history's most infamous individuals grace its confines. He made no speeches during his time in court, preferring that the prosecution did all the talking while he left his "not guilty" plea to speak for him. Harry "Big H" MacKenny hoped that the jury would believe the unbelievable – that he was not a mass murderer, but a lifesaver who had been framed.

At the end of his trial he leapt to his feet and screamed abuse and invective as the jury returned, beyond reasonable doubt, with guilty verdicts. Listening to the appalling catalogue of evidence stacked against him, it is inconceivable to believe that MacKenny could have conned himself into thinking that it could have gone any other way for him.

HE LEAPT TO HIS FEET AND SCREAMED ABUSE AND INVECTIVE AS THE JURY RETURNED GUILTY VERDICTS

Opposite: ***John Henry Childs, the killer who cracked and turned Queen's Evidence against the comrades in crime.***

Below: ***The flat where victims were turned from corpses to ashes.***

The macabre story began in a small fireplace in a small flat in a grimy part of East London, barely enough for more than one or two logs at a time. Outside, washing strung on the walkway of the flats fluttered in the breeze while dirty kids kicked a ball and tin cans around in the concrete play area outside the entrances. Inside flat 13 in Dolphin House, High Street, Poplar, the coals burned down to red hot embers. John Childs, the tenant of the overheated apartment, slugged whisky straight from a bottle. He handed it to Harry "Big H" MacKenny, who drank a deep draught, savouring the hot liquid as it burned on the way down before spreading a warm, mellow feeling throughout him. It was not a social drink. The men needed this liquor to steel themselves for the night's work ahead.

The fire, which was boosted with a gas burner to increase the heat, cast flickering, ominous shadows over the paraphernalia on the walls. Four knives, a pump-action shotgun, a shield, four axes, a crossbow, a pump-action air rifle, a compressed-air spear gun, Chinese flails and a fencing mask testified that the resident of this flat was a man who clearly dabbled in violence and violent things.

Childs, dressed in a weird black outfit that made him resemble a Victorian undertaker, put more smokeless fuel on to the grate as Big H went out to the back room. There Childs had installed an industrial mincing machine – bought for £25 from a wholesale butcher who advertised in Exchange and Mart magazine – a butcher's block, knives and hooks.

Hanging from the hooks were various human body parts. They had been dismembered earlier by Childs as he waited for Big H to come around and help him with the disposal of the corpse.

CALLOUS KILLERS

Piece by piece, as if carting home a joint for Sunday lunch, Big H carried through the human remains to Childs in the sitting room. The fire reached maximum heat and, for the next eighteen hours, the flames were fed with flesh and bone, fat drained off, the bones broken with mallets, the ash put into plastic bags to be finally scattered to the four winds by MacKenny as Childs drove them along the Barking by-pass in East London. The whisky blotted out the awful reality of what they were doing… the contract killings they specialised in for £25 down payment and easy instalments for the balance. They called themselves Murder Inc., and before they were caught half-a-dozen people were murdered for the paltry sum of a few thousand pounds.

Murder Inc. actually went on to become a triumvirate of misfits, although it was Childs and MacKenny who did all the killing. The third villain, who would eventually join Big H and Childs in the dock at the Old Bailey, in November 1980, was Terence Pinfold, a petty criminal and failed bank robber. An outsider in the terrible alliance of MacKenny and Childs, he was a hypocritical, weak man with the failing of most paranoid power lovers; he thought himself a cut above the other two and would become enraged if he thought they were laughing at him behind his back. Together they killed, for discount prices, using guns, a swordstick and an axe, dismembering the corpses at Childs' flat or at a disused factory in Chadwell Heath, Essex, that had once been used for manufacturing teddy bears.

Above: ***A Teddy Bear of the sort manufactured by Terence Eve.***

Opposite top: ***The unprepossessing base where Murder Inc. committed their crimes.***

Opposite bottom: ***The farm that was once owned by George Brett before he and 10-year-old son Terry were sten-gunned to death by Big H.***

The founding of this vile business came about when Pinfold and MacKenny became friends in the early 1970s. In 1972, at a factory in Chadwell Heath, they began making teddy bears with another man, Terence 'Teddy Bear' Eve. A secondary line at the factory was lifejackets. Although MacKenny was a psychotic killer, he was also an enigma, a talented, self-taught man who was a first class diver and qualified pilot. He once invented a unique diver's valve that was hailed in the trade press as a breakthrough and a life-jacket which incorporated the best points of six other types of

Above: ***The interior of the Teddy Bear factory where George Brett and his 10-year-old son Terry were murdered.***

A SEEDY, SMALL-TIME CROOK, PINFOLD BUNGLED EVERYTHING HE DID, FROM BURGLARY TO ARMED ROBBERY

life preserver. He drastically cut the weight of the existing systems by converting the diver's oxygen cylinder so that it would also inflate the life-jacket. The old method used a separate cylinder for the job.

At the factory the men grandly called themselves 'directors' and dressed in snazzy suits. But MacKenny was extremely lazy, refusing to rise much before midday each day, and soon the life-jacket business began, slowly but surely, to slide. The stuffed toys business, however, under the direction of Eve, continued to thrive with orders from all over the country. It was his success which would eventually lead him to becoming a victim.

It's clear at which point MacKenny turned the corner from legitimate businessman to murderer; it occurred in 1974 with the release from jail of John Childs.

Childs had known MacKenny in East London for several years, and had been friendly in the late 1960s in prison with Pinfold who was serving time for a robbery. A seedy, small-time crook, he had been in court on no less than 17 occasions and had served three jail sentences. From burglary to armed robbery, he bungled everything he did, but he always harboured the ambition to become a kingpin of crime in the East End, just like the Kray twins Reg and Ron whose reputation he admired so much. He also pulled a bank robbery once with Pinfold in south Woodford, Essex, saving Pinfold from capture when he was attacked by two bank staff after he failed to draw out his Walther .38 automatic in time to threaten them. They fled empty handed from that botched affair.

Childs was not even his real name. He was born Martin Jones, but took on the pseudonym when he rented the £6 per-week flat which he planned to turn into the human abattoir. A deeply unhinged psychopath, he liked to pull his own toenails out with a pair of pliers when dark moods overcame him. His greatest fantasy was – and still is, by all accounts – to have a waxwork model of himself repose in Madame Tussaud's in Baker Street.

The two of them formed their macabre new business. Each had contacts in the underworld on both sides of the Thames; each knew that they were all capable of going ahead. For discount prices – £25 to £50 down and easy repayments on the balance – they would take human life. Pinfold, reluctantly, was drawn in.

Before the first contract killing, Childs murdered Terence Eve, the man whose soft toy business was thriving. Early in 1975 he shot him dead with an automatic pistol, took MacKenny with him to the Poplar flat, and spent 14 hours burning Eve's corpse in a grate as the pair of them drank a litre of whisky. Pinfold, who never murdered, was later found guilty at the Old Bailey of ordering the killing and jailed for life. The jury were convinced that his greed harnessed Childs' macabre talents for the job.

SMALL-FRY

In February of that same year they received their first contract for £1,800 – a pathetically small sum compared to the fees charged by international, professional hitmen. The target was George Brett, a haulage contractor who lived on a farm in Upminster, Essex. Brett was on the fringes of the underworld – a dodgy deal here, a suspect load there – but was not a big-time criminal. But somewhere along the line, George Brett had crossed the line when his enemies learned that he had started 'grassing' them up to police as a paid informer. He was marked for death and the bargain-basement killing team were the perfect instrument to use.

Childs, a man obsessed with weapons and with a theatrical air about him, donned a wig, heavy eyebrows and dyed his straggly beard with black boot polish when he went to meet Brett to propose a lucrative business deal. Within a mile of his farmhouse he parked his car, stripped down to a tracksuit and ran along the roadside, pretending to be a jogger. When he "accidentally" bumped into Mrs. Brett, he got chatting and told her he was a engineer whose firm needed transport. She arranged a meeting with her husband who was "just the man you're looking for".

A killing zone was arranged at the factory. Tarpaulin sheets lined with plastic, to collect blood, were laid out in an area at the back of the site. Childs went back to the farm the following day dressed as a city gent to bring Brett to the factory. At the very last minute, just as he was manoeuvring his car out of the yard, Brett's young son Terence, aged 10, ran across. "Dad, can I come along for the ride?" he said, pleadingly. The boy climbed into the car for the last journey of his short life.

A DEEPLY UNHINGED PSYCHOPATH, HE LIKED TO PULL HIS OWN TOENAILS OUT WITH A PAIR OF PLIERS IN HIS DARK MOODS

Below: ***The police hunt at Beredens Farm for George and Terry Brett.***

Above: ***At Beredens Farm a large section of the farmyard was dug up as police looked for the bodies.***

into smaller pieces and once again burned in the 18-inch-wide grate. It is still now known how much they charged for that particular contract killing.

A chilling insight into the menace they generated was provided by Mike Fielder, a veteran crime reporter for The Sun, who visited the death factory for a story about the disappearance of Eve. He said: "I came face to face with the killers in their factory of death. Pinfold told me that Eve had vanished with £600 in takings and had got 'a bit of woman trouble'.

"As we talked both MacKenny, 6 ft 5 ins tall and an unmistakeable figure, and Childs hovered nearby without joining in the conversation.

"Pinfold stonewalled every question. I got a guided tour of the factory from Pinfold.

At the factory he was held by Childs while watching his father's head blown off with a silenced Sten gun by Big H. Then the boy was cut in half by bullets fired from the same gun. As he looked at the boy's corpse MacKenny said: "It don't matter – he's only a grass's son." They were cut up, taken in plastic bin liners to Child's flat and burned. Then their ashes were thrown from the moving car. They had simply vanished from the face of the earth. Except for one of 35-year-old George Brett's eyes... MacKenny took it from his corpse with the intention of preserving it in vinegar.

AT THE FACTORY THE BOY WAS HELD BY CHILDS WHILE WATCHING HIS FATHER'S HEAD BEING BLOWN OFF

The rubicon had been crossed. Killing for cash, they thought, was this simple.

The next to die was Frederick Sherwood, proprietor of a nursing home in Herne Bay, Kent. Sherwood, 48, was wanted out of the way by a business rival keen on muscling in on his lucrative enterprise. MacKenny discovered his car was for sale and lured him there on the pretext of being interested in buying it for £480. When Sherwood arrived the same killing zone had been prepared and he was shot through the head by MacKenny at the same time as Childs smashed a sledge-hammer over him. At the factory his legs were sawn off, the body complete with dismembered limbs taken to Childs' flat where it was sawed and hacked

MACKENNY TOOK ONE OF GEORGE BRETT'S EYES FROM HIS CORPSE WITH THE INTENTION OF PRESERVING IT IN VINEGAR

"He showed me the teddy bear production line and how the toys were stuffed with foam rubber. Then he cheekily asked for my help in trying to prove that he had been 'framed' by the police on a £20,000 bank raid charge. At the time he said he had just been granted bail while awaiting trial. I said I would make a few enquiries on his behalf. But I felt in my bones that Pinfold was an evil and dangerous man. I never returned to the factory. And if I had known then what the world knows now, I would not have slept easy in my bed that night. A prying newspaperman would have made a tempting target for murder."

ANOTHER BRUTAL KILLING

Robert Brown, 36, an escaped prisoner who ended up working at the factory, was the next victim. He was killed with an axe by Childs because he "irritated him", and, like the others, disposed of in the grate.

While they touted for murders, MacKenny and Childs also drew up a lurid "shopping list" among the underworld of the kind of "services" that their organisation was offering. For £50 they would break someone's nose. For £500 they would blow kneecaps off with a shotgun. And for two grand – £2,000 – they would kill. They offered to help slum landlords deal with bothersome tenants by slipping diseased rats through letterboxes and they touted their talents to the right-wing National Front party – promising to deal with "troublesome Pakis" if they so wished. They even hit on the hare-brained idea that Lord Lucan, the runaway peer wanted for the murder of his nanny in Belgravia, was still alive, so they offered his relatives bargain-basement contracts on anyone who showed "malevolence" towards the Earl! The offer was never taken seriously. Another person they approached was the self-confessed racialist Robert Relf, the 56-year-old white supremacist who had gone to jail in Leamington for refusing to take down a sign which offered his house for sale to a white person only. Relf would later tell police: "MacKenny thought I would be a good customer. They thought I had a lot of black enemies that I wanted to dispose of. MacKenny put it to me that if I had any bother with coloureds he would get them 'seen to'. He said they could either get rid of them altogether or just frighten them off like break their arms and legs – for a price. I told him I wasn't interested. I know I'm a racialist but I'm not going for things like that – not with any violence."

THEY SLIPPED DISEASED RATS THROUGH LETTERBOXES AND OFFERED THEIR SERVICES TO THE NATIONAL FRONT

A VICIOUS FRIEND

The next, and last, victim was Ronald Andrews – a man killed over MacKenny's lust for his wife. Andrews, 35, a roofing contractor, was MacKenny's best friend, a man he had known since his childhood days in Camberwell. But twice-married MacKenny, always a lady's man, did not let friendship stand in the way of what he wanted. He had been carrying on an affair for some time with his wife, Gwen, deciding, with the aid of Childs to murder him in the autumn of 1978.

MacKenny lured him to the DIY crematorium in Poplar on the pretext of introducing him to a private detective who alleged-

Below: ***The farm was pulled apart as the police conducted the most thorough of searches.***

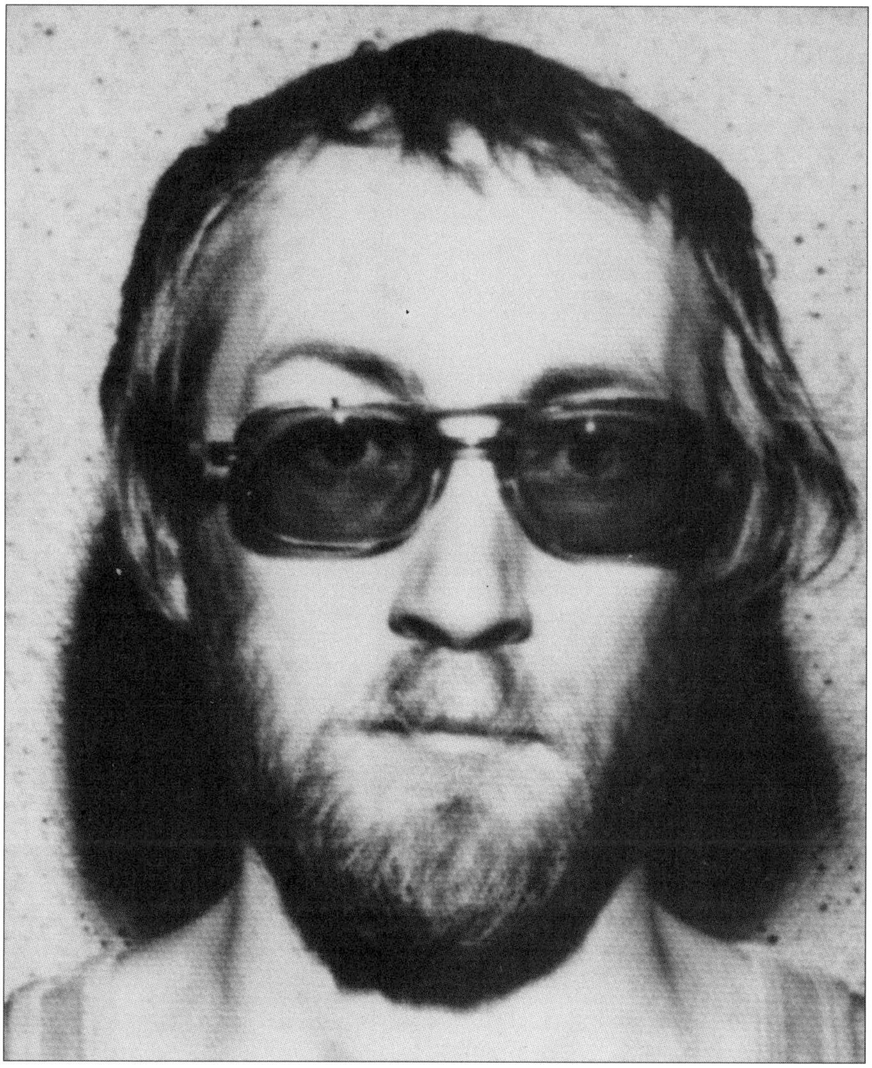

ly had information on affairs his wife was having with other men. The private detective turned out to be Childs. Andrews was lulled into a false sense of security, being offered tea by MacKenny who then went out into the kitchen, pretending to have a conversation with "Mrs. Childs", although in reality there was no-one else there.

Concealing a .38 revolver under a tea-towel he came back in, ripped the towel away, and shot him point blank through the back of the skull. Then his body was sawed up into log-size pieces, parts of it grated down in the industrial mincer and the flesh burned in the grate. Childs had to drink two bottles of whisky… his nerves were close to cracking.

To cover up the killing Childs had got his ex-wife to write a loving postcard to "Dear Ron", which was posted from Wisbech, Cambridgeshire, to his wife – MacKenny wanted it to appear to her that her husband was the cheat. He drove Andrews' car to the River Nene and dumped it in the black waters. Wearing frogman's gear, he waited until the car completely filled up with water before breaking out and swimming to the surface. He hoped that police would think that the body had been swept away by the current. Days later, when Ron Andrews was already ashes, MacKenny stood with Gwendoline on the banks of the river and comforted her as the car was dragged up from the depths.

Above: ***The defendants were desperate men.***

Right: ***Henry 'Big H' MacKenny, one of the vilest killers ever to stand trial for multiple murder.***

HIS BODY WAS SAWED INTO LOG-SIZE PIECES, PARTS OF IT GRATED DOWN IN THE INDUSTRIAL MINCER. FLESH BURNED IN THE GRATE

PAYING THE PRICE FOR EVIL

By this time, Childs' nerves were almost completely shot. He had grown sleepless, wracked by nightmares about the terrible things he had done. He was now drinking at least one bottle, sometimes two, of whisky each night, merely to blot out the memories to get some sleep. He would later tell police that he had, in his paranoia, become convinced that MacKenny was out to kill him. He wanted to get the first shot in and began practising with pictures of MacKenny tied to a tree in Epping Forest that he took pot-shots at with a crossbow.

MacKenny, too, began to question some of the murders, particularly the killing of Andrews. In one moment of remorse he

said to Childs: "I shouldn't have done that. He was my best mate." But he was nowhere near as close-to-the-edge as his partner... although time was rapidly running out for them both.

Police had been probing the disappearances of all the victims, but had nothing to tie them in – until the end of 1978 when a suspect wanted for a string of armed robberies in the home counties began talking of an underworld hit team. Villains all over knew of the gruesome speciality of Childs and MacKenny, but true to their criminal code, they stayed silent.

This particular suspect named Childs and MacKenny, although to police it seemed almost impossible to prove. For if what the crook was saying, there would be no bodies, no forensic evidence, to ever link them with the crimes.

The squad assigned to cracking the case was led by Det. Chief Supt. Frank Cater, later Commander Cater, a lawman with an outstanding record of success against organised crime in the capital. His second-in-command was Det. Insp. Geoffrey Foxall, responsible for co-ordinating operations and all relevant information in the murder squad incident room. With information from a further two informers, a 20-strong task force called Cater's Company began the task of seeking hard evidence to back up the uncorroborated statements of criminals.

Above: ***The Volkswagen which led police on a high-speed chase and the capture of Big H.***
Below: ***The Barking by-pass, resting place for many of Big H's murder victims.***

CRIMINAL LINKS

Childs was arrested for questioning over a £500,000 security van robbery in Hertfordshire in the summer of 1979. But he soon realised he had been offered up by a "squealer" for something far more damaging than mere armed robberies or grievous bodily harm. With his nerve completely broken, he turned supergrass, confessing to six killings, detailing every single gruesome episode. The hardened detectives could simply not believe that human beings could be so thoroughly disposed of in an 18-inch-grate in a council flat. So to test the theory two officers were assigned the task of burning an 11-and-a-half-stone pig in the flat. They had reduced the animal to ashes in 13 hours, pulverised its bones and disposed of the ashes from a car on the Barking by-pass – just like Childs and MacKenny had done. Childs hoped that his full confession would be enough to earn him a pardon. He was sadly mistaken.

With detectives sent to interview all the associates of the missing people, tracking down the places where they drank and where they placed their bets, forensic evi-

Above: ***The blue Mercedes which George Brett and his son Terry drove in their appointment with brutal murder.***

They came to trial at the Old Bailey in October 1980 – the largest mass murder case ever to be brought where no victims had ever been discovered. For close to two months the jury listened to what judge Mr. Justice May called "a story I have seldom heard even in these violent times."

MacKenny and Pinfold were in the dock, their erstwhile business partner and cohort in crime John Childs paraded before them as their chief prosecution witness. Childs left nothing out. He detailed every gory move that he and MacKenny had made. Pinfold was made to look weak and pathetic; even though he wanted Terence Eve dead, Childs had to confess that he did not take part in the killing. He told the court: "I live in fear of my life now. I was a professional criminal and I have broken the code."

dence proved more difficult. A search of the teddy bear factory showed only an area where large amounts of concentrated acid had been poured to remove bloodstains. But there was one mark in the floor which corresponded to the tip of a bullet that had been disguised with the aid of polish and wax. It was the first small, but significant clue, that would eventually lead to the downfall of Murder Inc.

THE BIG SEARCH

In July 1979 a massive dragnet was set up by police to find MacKenny. But he too had his underworld contacts. He realised that he had been sold out by Childs and had gone to ground, and managed to elude capture despite a massive poster campaign combined with radio and TV appeals. He was eventually found to be staying at a house in Morse Close, Plaistow, East London, the home of his friends William and Pauline Woodcraft.

A large team of armed officers, wearing bullet-proof vests, ringed the house, evacuating some neighbours while telling others to keep quiet and stay indoors. Shortly after 1.00 a.m. on September 21, police telephoned the house, spoke to Mrs. Woodcraft, and told her that the place was surrounded. MacKenny, realising the hopelessness of the situation, came out without a shot being fired.

THE TRIAL AT THE OLD BAILEY WAS THE LARGEST MASS MURDER CASE WHERE NO VICTIMS HAD EVER BEEN DISCOVERED

TWO DETECTIVES ON THE SQUAD WERE UNDER CONSTANT FEAR OF THEIR LIVES FROM ANOTHER UNDERWORLD CONTRACT

For their part, the police revealed how two detectives who were on the squad which cracked the case were under constant fear of their lives from another underworld contract, put out on them by acquaintances of MacKenny while they delved into their murders.

Big H, defiant to the end, insisted he was a life-saver, the inventor of the life-jacket and breathing apparatus at the factory, not a cold-blooded killer. But John Childs' description of his callous remark over the dead body of 10-year-old Terry Brett virtually froze the courtroom.

He was convicted of murdering the Bretts, Eve and Frederick Sherwood and jailed for four life terms, concurrently, with Mr. Justice May recommending that he serve not less than 25 years. The pitiful Pinfold, the outsider in the drama who just got greedy over wanting the teddy bear factory for himself, was sentenced to life imprisonment for ordering Eve's murder.

DRAMATIC SCENES

There were scenes of high drama in the heavily guarded courtroom on Friday November 28 1980 as the judge came to sentence MacKenny. He told him: "The public needs to be protected from your criminal and totally unjustified activities." MacKenny, tall, greying, dressed in a cream suit, shouted back: "Straight people need to be protected from you." The judge, ignoring this outburst as prison officers restrained him, said: "This is one of the most macabre cases ever heard, even in this famous building." Again MacKenny interrupted: "I think you are a hypocrite. Bring this farce to a close. Do your worst. I killed nobody. I have saved lives!" The Judge said, as he was surrounded in the dock by yet more prison officers: "You have killed for no reason whatever – two for gain and one your best friend because you wanted his wife." Big H then began a torrent of abuse and swear words, his invective echoing all the way down to the cells as he was led away to begin his 25 years locked away from civilised society.

BIG H BEGAN A TORRENT OF ABUSE AND SWEAR WORDS, HIS INVECTIVE ECHOING ALL THE WAY DOWN TO THE CELLS

Psychopath Childs was sentenced to life with little hope of ever seeing the world outside of an institution ever again. But even from behind bars the hot breath of his menace can still be felt. In August 1983 he attempted, from his cell at Hull maximum security prison, to write the memoirs of Murder Inc. On prison notepaper he wrote to Redbridge council, the local authority which gave planning permission for the teddy bear factory. He asked for the council to send him the plans of the factory for one of his chapters. The council had to treat the request "like any other". But an official said: "We feel like telling him to get lost. He certainly has a nerve."

The Home Office had the final say. Institution rules forbid inmates of Her Majesty's Prisons from profiting from such ventures and he will never be allowed to have his grisly memoirs published while he languishes inside. Instead, he can console himself that he might, indeed, one day end up immortalised in the chamber of horrors at Madame Tussaud's.

Below: ***The Old Bailey, where a jury decided, beyond reasonable doubt, that the killers who made up Murder Inc. needed to be put away from society.***

ROOM 606
A Race Case

Mike Tyson, the man with the meanest fists on the planet, became a number in the system when he was found guilty of rape and sentenced to time in a tough jail. It was the worst setback for world-class boxing in years, a tragedy for his victim, and a blow to the black community in America who idolised him.

The bathing-suit belles giggled nervously in their skimpy suits, wobbling on their high heels as their hero hove into view. Mike Tyson, ex-heavyweight boxing champion of the world, was even more awesome close-up than he was on the screen punching his opponents to kingdom come. Tyson, a born-again bachelor since his highly publicised divorce from actress Robin Givens two years before, moved at ease among the beauties, aware of both his physical appeal and his incredible stature among the black communities of America. And these girls were all his "own" – black girls competing in an all-black beauty pageant at an exposition in the midwestern city of Indianapolis in 1991.

"How ya doin baby?" grinned Tyson to one girl after another. Sometimes the comments were much lewder, much cruder, but some of these girls were from the ghetto like Tyson – they both understood and spoke the language of the streets. Few were

THESE GIRLS WERE ALL HIS "OWN"... "HOW YA DOIN' BABY?" GRINNED MIKE TYSON AT ONE GIRL AFTER ANOTHER

Opposite: ***Mike Tyson, a champion humbled.***

Below: ***Before Tyson's problems with Desiree Washington began, his shattered marriage to actress Robin Givens was played out in public – much to his discomfort.***

Above: ***Mike Tyson and his flamboyant manager Don King, on top of the world after winning a world title fight in Las Vegas in 1987.***

IT BECAME CLEAR TO A WATCHING WORLD THAT HE WAS A BRUTISH MAN WHO TOOK WHAT HE WANTED WHEN HE WANTED IT

offended by the boxer's purple language and sexist remarks.

One 18-year-old among the contestants that day was particularly overawed at being in the presence of boxing's maestro. Desiree Washington, a vivacious beauty, a scholar, a girl from a nice middle-class home, didn't hear the risque banter; she just hoped with baited breath that the man idolised by her entire family would stop to speak with her. He did – and their separate worlds ended. For Mike Tyson, champ, became Mike Tyson, rapist. For the next few years he was destined to languish in a maximum security American jail.

Tyson exchanged telephone numbers with the girl from Rhode Island and they met later that night for what she thought was going to be a nice sightseeing tour of the bright lights of Indianapolis. Her tour, however, ended in room 606 of the plush Canterbury Hotel where Tyson raped her in an ordeal that has scarred her mentally for life. Tyson proclaimed his innocence throughout the ensuing trial, but it became clear to a watching world that he was a brutish man who took what he wanted when he wanted it. Certainly for the jurors who sat in judgement on him there was only ever going to be one verdict when the ten days of the trial were over – guilty beyond reasonable doubt.

A SHOW TRIAL

From the first day prosecutor Greg Garrison spoke the world knew that this was going to be an incredible trial. Two hundred journalists from around the world were accommodated in an underground storeroom at the courthouse where the trial proceedings were relayed to them on closed-circuit TV. Garrison, setting the scene for his portrayal of Tyson as a predatory beast, said that he had 'lured' her to his hotel room, violated her and discarded her afterwards like so much trash.

The hushed court on the first day of proceedings heard that hours before the attack he had knelt in prayer with the Rev. Jesse Jackson. But after midnight, the lust for the young beauty he had met earlier in the day welled up inside him. Garrison said that the attraction between the former champ and the beauty queen changed from innocence to a nightmare rape ordeal in a split second on July 19 1991.

"She was asleep when Tyson phoned to invite her for a ride around town in his limousine," said Garrison. "He told her he was leaving town the next day. So she gets up and decides to go and see the town with one of her heroes. She was excited. She thought: 'I am out on the town with Mike Tyson!' But then he said something about having to go back to his hotel, something about bodyguards, something about making phone calls.

"On the way into the hotel a 13-year-old girl yelled out: 'Hey, there's Mike Tyson,' and he waved back. Desiree says to him: 'It's great you are doing this,' but he replies: 'Yeah, but it's a pain in the ass.'

"Once in the room she goes and sits on the first chair and he walks through to the living room in the two-room suite. She hears him talking on the phone but doesn't hear what he is saying. He shouts: 'Come in, I want to talk to you.'

"She says: 'I thought we were going to go out on the town.' He replied: 'We will go, come in, I want to talk to you.' When she goes in he is sitting at the head of the bed watching a cowboy show on TV. He says to her: 'Does your family like me?' She says: 'They don't know you.' He then says: 'Well, do you like me?' And she replied: 'You seem nice.'

"And he changed in a second. There was a change in his voice and in his actions. He said to her: 'You are 18 years and one month old and you turn me on.' She says: 'What? Now look, I don't know what you think I came up here for, but you said we would see the sights and I brought my camera. I want to go to the bathroom and then go.' Tyson then held his head in his hands, rubbed his eyes, and said that he would take her back to his hotel after she had been to the lavatory.

"But when she came out of the bathroom he was sitting on the edge of the bed with nothing on but his underpants and he said to her: 'Come here.' Then one of the fastest and strongest men in the world grabbed and spun around this 18-year-old girl as she said: 'What are you doing to me?'

AN UNFAIR STRUGGLE

"He then pins her on the bed and sticks his tongue halfway down her throat. She begs him to get off. A massive forearm pins her down like a ragdoll and he peels her clothes off with one hand. She begs the heavweight champion of the world to get off her. He pulls her legs apart and she cries out in pain. She is tearful. She is frightened. She hurts a lot and says to him: 'Please, I don't want to have a baby.'

"He says: 'We'll have a baby together.' She says: 'I cannot afford to have a baby. I cannot get any diseases.' Tyson replied: 'I have not got any diseases and neither have you.' And he screams at her: 'Don't fight me, don't fight me!' Like a ragdoll he lifts her up. He exposes himself, drives himself into this 5ft. 4ins. 18-year-old girl. She says: 'You are hurting me. Please don't do this to me.' She is hitting him but she later says it is like hitting a brick wall. He goes on until he is done. She is crying all the while, begging him to get up."

The courtroom remained transfixed as Garrison described how Desiree tried to make a bolt for freedom when Tyson suggested she sit on top of him for more sex. "She makes a break from the bed," he said, "but he grabs her back and forces himself on her again until he climaxes. Then in an eerie voice he says to her: 'You love me now, don't you?' Tearful, Desiree staggered from the room. Back in her hotel room her

Above: ***Desiree Washington, the beauty queen who accepted an invitation to see the sights of Indianapolis with Mike Tyson… and ended up as his victim in a rape without mercy.***

Above: ***The gloves and boxer shorts have been swapped for an Armani suit and silk tie as Mike Tyson prepares to fight for something far more important than purses or titles – his freedom and his name.***

roomate asked: 'What was he like?' And Desiree replied: 'He raped me.'" Garrison said she complained to police a day later and when doctors examined her, they found two wounds "clearly visible 25 hours after the attack. It is beyond reasonable doubt that he callously and viciously raped her."

Tyson's lawyer, a tax expert for his manager Don King called Vincent Fuller, embarked on a weird strategy to try to defend his client from such shattering testimony. Rather than painting Tyson as the victim of a financial sting or a girl who cried wolf because he was not more romantic, he went on the tack of portraying Tyson as a brute. Yes, he was tough, he was crude, he was brutal – but girls KNEW that because he was from the ghetto. His bottom line was that any girl who went into a hotel room after midnight with a hulk like Tyson should have known they weren't going there to play scrabble. "There is no denial on Mr. Tyson's part that sex took place," he said. "But we will prove that sex was consensual." He argued that Miss Washington had a craving for cash equal to that of his ex-wife Robin Givens, a woman who took him to the financial cleaners after they split up. And he says the fact that Tyson didn't call a cab after the brief encounter led her to concoct the rape story. He added: "Miss Washington left his room in anger – not because of rape, but because of disillusionment."

"I ASKED HER IF SHE WANTED TO F**K ME THE FIRST TIME I MET HER," HE SAID. "SHE REPLIED: 'SURE – GIVE ME A CALL'"

Tyson did nothing on the witness stand to endear himself to the jurors or the judge. He swore, he spoke in crude terms of what he did to women, he frequently blurted out the F-word. "I asked her if she wanted to f***k me the first time I met her," he said. "She repled: 'Sure – give me a call.' I am very blunt, very crude. That's what I am when I ask for something – I want to know what I am getting." He said that far from being an innocent victim, a Sunday school teacher in her hometown, she "thrust" her telephone number into his hand when he had met her earlier in the day at the beauty contest. He said he made several telephone calls to her hotel before finally getting through to her shortly before midnight. He claimed she told him: "S**t, I'm in bed and have got no make-up." Tyson said: "I told her to just wash her face, comb her hair and just put on something loose. When she came down to the car there was just my driver there and my bodyguard Dale Edwards. I kissed her and she kissed me. We were kissing and touching, you know.

BEDROOM TALK

"We went to the bedroom of my hotel and we started talking. We were talking for about ten minutes, perhaps, and we were touching, my hand was on her leg. Yeah, we were kissing. I slid down the bed to reach her and she's movin' fast, dropping her jacket, getting it off quick. I was kissing her neck, her cheeks, kissing her chest, kissing her shoulders and her nipples. She had taken off her shorts and I had taken my shirt off. She had taken off her underwear and the underwear had dropped to her knees and then I took it all off. I started having oral sex with her. We had oral sex for a little while. She told me to stop, saying 'come up, come up.' That indicated she wanted sex. We had sex. It lasted for 15 or 20 minutes. She was not on the pill so I didn't climax inside her.

"I offered her to stay the night because she and a girlfriend had a 5.00am wake-up call. I said my limo would take her home but that I was not going to walk back down the stairs. She was irritable because I would not walk her down the stairs."

Fuller interrupted his client's monologue to ask Tyson: "At any time did you force Desiree Washington to engage in sexual

"SHE WANTED SEX. WE HAD SEX. SHE WAS NOT ON THE PILL SO I DIDN'T CLIMAX INSIDE HER"

Below: ***Camille Ewald, the elderly white woman who raised Mike Tyson as her own son since his teens, was one of the few women in America who stood by him and spoke out for him at his rape trial.***

Above: ***This is what Mike Tyson did best – hammering opponents into mincemeat with his terrible fury.***

"SOME OF THE THINGS THAT WERE SAID PAINTED ME AS A MANIAC, A GUY GOING CRAZY. BUT I WAS JUST TRYING TO HAVE FUN"

"IT WAS HORRIBLE TO BE IN THIS COURTROOM... TOTALLY UNBELIEVABLE... I AM DEVASTATED... I WAS CRUCIFIED"

intercourse?" Tyson replied: "No, I did not. Never. I did not violate her in any way." "Did she tell you to stop?" inquired Fuller. Tyson responded emotionally: "Never! She never told me I was hurting her, she never said no or anything."

Desiree on the stand was treated with kid-gloves by prosecution and defence alike. She merely re-stated what Garrison had said in his opening arguments and Fuller could do little other than suggest that sex was consensual. There followed a stream of other witnesses, including other beauty queens, all of whom testified as to the lewd and licencious nature of Tyson's comments to the contestants that morning. But it was clear that the proceedings were not going his way. After deliberating at trial's end for nine hours and 20 minutes the verdict came in: guilty of rape.

A STRONG SPEECH

In his last moments as Mike Tyson, free man, before he became prisoner no. 922355, Tyson showed no remorse in the dock. Instead he gave a dramatic 12 minute speech in which he protested his innocence and expressed disbelief at what had happened to him. He said: "I would like to apologise for the things that have been said in this court. Some of the things I agreed with, some of the things I do not agree with. I have been convicted but I did not rape anyone. I did not attempt to rape anyone. I am sorry – I agree that I did something but I did not mean to do it. My conduct when I went to Indianapolis was kind of crass, I agree.

"Some of the things that were said painted me as a maniac, a guy going crazy. But I was just trying to have fun. I don't know why a complaint was made against me because we talked back and forth and made agreements. The situation happened and I cannot believe she said what she said.

"It is incredible to believe how I could fool her and do these horrific things to her. I am sorry not only for me but also for my family and the people close to me. People said I had been manipulated by money but I read the papers – I can read the papers – and some of the things that were said about me were not very nice. I am not vindictive or ferocious. Things that were said by the prosecution were very distasteful." Then, pointing at prosecution tormentor Garrison he said: "He was on TV. He was on the Barbara Walters show. These flash-in-the-pan media stars making comments on incidents they have no knowledge of. Big man – he was on Barbara Walters. I was hurt. I was humiliated. I expect the worst here today. I don't know if I can deal with it but I am not afraid because I am not guilty. I did not hurt anyone.

"She had no black eyes, no broken ribs. I am not the type. They said I was emotionally disturbed. I don't know what emotionally disturbed is. Charles Manson – I guess he's emotionally disturbed. My life has been incarcerated by this. I am a public figure and this goes worldwide. It was horrible to be in this courtroom, one big dream, totally unbelievable. I am devastated – not just for myself but for the people who support me. I cannot see any good coming out of it. I was crucified. The reason I don't cry is that the people standing behind me are stronger than I. I feel that if I cry I will lose them. I am prepared to deal with this. That's all that I am prepared to say."

As Judge Patricia Gifford pronounced sentence of six years she told him: "I believe there are two Mike Tysons – one capable of kindness and generosity and one that acts in the manner which you did in Indianapolis last year." Tyson, surrounded by four prison guards, rose slowly from his seat. He took off his gold watch and cufflinks, handed them to his lawyer and then walked slowly away from the courtroom and into incarceration.

Yet even as a free man he will be guilty – as the court says he is – or innocent as he maintains he is. Perhaps for Desiree, her sentence is one for life. After the trial she said: "I feel no happiness or elation about this. I am saddened however that Tyson showed no remorse or regret. I thought I would have a sense of relief that it is all over, but I don't. I feel in a sombre mood, almost down. This is still very difficult for me to deal with. I fear it will leave a permanent scar. But I will just have to get on with being a college kid again."

TOUGH TIMES

That has not been easy for Desiree in the years since Tyson has languished behind the bars of the Indiana Youth Centre – an innocuous sounding name for a maximum security jail. There are many in America who feel that Tyson got the rough end of the stick – particularly in the black community. Desiree has been every bit as much a prisoner as Tyson. She can go nowhere without the stares, the whispers, the accusing fingers that she plotted his downfall to get her painted nails into his fortune.

America's blacks, victims of a racist past and present that still pervades all aspects of their society, have branded her a female "Uncle Tom" – black on the outside but white on the inside. She bears the mark of Cain – bringing down a "brother" for "cracker-ass honkies" intent on keeping blacks in their place.

Private detectives have delved into the past which was strictly off-limits at the ten-day trial in February 1992. Resulting allegations suggested that violent rows with her father punctuated her upbringing – that once he tried to drown her after finding out she lost her virginity at 15. It was also alleged that she underwent psychiatric counselling after these rows. And the world also knows that now she plans to sue Mike

AMERICA'S BLACKS HAVE BRANDED HER A FEMALE "UNCLE TOM" – BLACK ON THE OUTSIDE BUT WHITE ON THE INSIDE

Below: ***Prison cost Mike Tyson everything – his titles, his respect, his money, his adulation and material comforts like this £3.5 million mansion outside Bernardsville, New Jersey.***

Left: ***An artist's impression of Desiree Washington giving firm and disturbing testimony against Tyson.***

Tyson for a large percentage of his not inconsiderable fortune. The sum of the parts of that, and other lurid portions of her background, is meant to equal this: that Desiree Washington was sexually experienced, slightly unbalanced, and financially motivated when she walked into room 606 after midnight with Mike Tyson, her hero.

Her detractors say that these allegations show she set him up for a fall.

Rape counsellors and feminists are appalled by the treatment that has marked Desiree out as a social leper. And they point to the effectivness of the campaign to rubbish her by the fact that two of the jurors who convicted Tyson now say they believe she was NOT raped. "It is incredible to think that the weight of public opinion has been manipulated in this fashion," said Renee Dodds, a rape crisis centre organiser in Los Angeles. "She gave her testimony and he was convicted of rape. Now we have all this extra-court kangaroo justice whereby it seems fair and right to trawl through her past to make judgements on her and her motives. The jury decided then that there was no motive on her part. She was RAPED. And now she is being punished for it. Never have I seen less sympathy for a proven victim of rape."

Punishment is how Desiree sees it too. A student at a college in Providence, Rhode Island, she shuns the out-of-classroom activities which she once enjoyed so much. There are no more beauty pageants, like the one where she met Tyson, to be attended. There are no more dances to go to, no movies to share with boyfriends. In statements issued through lawyers she said: "I am the victim yet I am also the guilty one. It seems I am being punished for this. My life was destroyed that day and yet people are always trying to prove Mike Tyson innocent. He knows what he did. I don't hate him, but I do think he has to pay for what he did. God knows that I am paying for what he did. Some people have turned against me. His people have portrayed me as scheming and manupulative.

Below: ***The verdict is in and Mike Tyson leaves the court with his lawyer Vincent Fuller.***

"But I told the truth that night. I said no and he raped me. I know the support he has in the black community by the fact that I was offered money before the trial to drop the charges. I was offered a million dollars. If I wanted just money why didn't I say yes and not go ahead with it? I had to go ahead with it because I was brought up to do what's right. But my life will never be the same. Never."

A PERSONALITY CHANGE

Friends who know her say she has changed beyond all recognition. The bright, bubbly personality has been transformed into one of sullen introspection. Her parents' marriage broke up shortly after the trial and she lives with her mother, Mary Bell Washington, who does her best to shield her daughter away from the worst excesses of anti-Desiree hysteria. Desiree herself cannot quite grasp that a huge segment of America's black population hates her for what she did. Black activist Nathan Pearson, who points out that he makes no judgement on Desiree, says: "They see her as a person who destroyed a black icon. You don't got much in the ghetto – you got dreams and heroes. Well, she took away a hero when she cried rape. And people think: 'What you doing, child, in a room with Mike Tyson at 2.00am if you ain't there for one thing?' Black people have got enough troubles without blacks turning on blacks. I think that is part of the problem with Desiree and the black community."

In the case of Indianapolis v Tyson, there are no winners – only losers.

Above: ***The jurors who put the world champ behind bars answer press questions.***

Below: ***The famous hands that floored his rivals are prepared for fingerprinting.***

KILLING GAMES
Unsporting conduct

Jayne Scott took a hammer to the head of her lesbian love rival and injured the woman she despised so much she became little more than a wheelchair-bound vegetable. Victim Susan Craker was a deputy headmistress, tangled up in a web of sexual intrigue spawned upon the playing fields of Eton and Windsor.

It was a sensational trial at the nation's premier court – the Old Bailey, London. In the dock stood a woman accused of grievous bodily harm, namely that attractive Jayne Scott had taken a claw hammer to the head of her lesbian love-rival and attacked her with such ferocity that the woman she despised was left as little more than a wheelchair-bound vegetable.

What added even more intrigue to the court case – as spicy and as lurid as Britain had witnessed in many a year – was that victim Susan Craker was a deputy headmistress, tangled up in a web of sexual intrigue spawned upon the playing fields of Eton and Windsor. British police in modern times have had their fair share of dealing with criminal conspiracies, but none seemed as strange, when it was unravelled, as that of the teachers who were linked in a blue-stocking network of lesbianism. "Secret Lust of the Netball Girls!" screamed the headline in one tabloid news-

IT WAS A COURT CASE AS SPICY AND LURID AS BRITAIN HAD WITNESSED IN MANY A YEAR

Opposite: ***Jayne Scott, whose jealousy led her to extreme violence.***

Below: ***The proximity of the famous Eton school brought unwelcome attention to the area.***

Above: ***Sue Craker, pictured before the attack which left her a virtual vegetable.***

GIRLS WHO COMPETED SO VIGOROUSLY ON THE SPORTS FIELD WERE BEDHOPPING, KISSING AND CUDDLING OFF IT

paper when the trial ended with Scott's conviction. The image of the jolly-hockey-sticks mistresses was changed forever in its wake. For those muscular girls who competed so vigorously in cricket, netball and hockey on the field were bedhopping, kissing and cuddling off of it. And their dangerous liaisons were to end with such tragic consequences for Susan Craker.

Jayne Scott was a teacher before she wound up standing before the full might of British justice at the Old Bailey in August 1986. A staff member at the 500-pupil Slough and Eton Church of England Secondary School, she was popular among pupils and staff alike in her position as gym mistress. She taught all the usual sports and served on a netball committee outside school hours. Her victim Sue Craker was not as popular among schoolchildren, probably because of her position close to supreme authority at the school as deputy headmistress. Janita Lake, a pupil who left in the same summer as the attack, said: "Miss Scott was great. She was the sort of woman you could go to and talk about anything with. She enjoyed a laugh and a joke and was everyone's favourite.

But Miss Craker was terrible. If you walked past her she would just give you a hard stare." That was an unfair viewpoint from someone who just knew her as a keeper of rules and discipline. Sue Craker was, at 36, a top all-round sportswoman, dynamic and ambitious, who excelled in cricket, squash and swimming and who was destined for the top of the academic ladder. And also what Janita did not know, nor the rest of the school, or her parents or anyone else save for a select few, was that both women were lesbians. Both kept the fact a secret from each other in the early days, but the world they moved in was small… and gossipy.

THE OBJECT OF DESIRE

Jayne Scott, at 31, was considered attractive by men at her school, but from her earliest years had been attracted to people of the same sex. The terrible tangled web which would lead to the ruination of Craker's life began being woven when she was attracted to married woman Debbie Fox. Debbie was a 34-year-old petite blonde, a sophisticated dresser who worked as credit controller. She was trapped in a "brother and sister" marriage and looked for gratification elsewhere. The court heard how Debbie, who described herself as bisexual, was on the same extra-curricular sporting committee as Jayne – the Slough and Eton Netball League. Debbie was about to split from her husband and had thrown herself into sports as one way of easing the pain of the break-up.

She later revealed: "I met Jayne and for months we just met as friends. But one weekend she invited me to a hockey tournament in Weymouth when she was playing for the Guildford Ladies team. I knew then that my feelings for her had changed,

Left and Below: ***Abbots Road and the house where the brutal attack that would lead to Jayne Scott's trial at the Old Bailey took place.***

but nothing happened. It was the first time I had had feelings like this for a woman. I told her I fancied her on a walk home but she said: 'But you're married!' We became lovers after a hockey tournament in Southampton. I took the dominant role." The passionate affair between the two women snowballed... with Debbie sneaking home to her husband after her sex sessions with Jayne.

But Debbie insisted: "Jayne was in no way responsible for the break-up of my marriage. My husband and I had talked about going our own ways long before that. When we split up I moved into a flat with her and we bought it on a joint mortgage."

Like most couples – certainly married ones – they settled into a life that was more routine than roaring passion. Debbie told the Old Bailey that Jayne soon began to rebuff her sexual advances and that they didn't have sex with each other for more than a year. Then, because of her involvement with sports, she met Susan Craker and became attracted to her. Craker was herself involved in a domestic gay situation – she lived with lesbian shoe-shop manageress Kate Potts, 34, and was also on the lookout for sexual gratification from somewhere else. The catalyst for the dangerous liaison between Craker and Fox came when the four gay girls went together on a Riverboat Shuffle – a disco down the Thames organised by the school where the teachers were based. Afterwards, at a house in Windsor, the foursome carried on their own private party.

Fox told the court that she had danced with Kate Potts and Sue Craker but that her own live-in lover Scott turned her down. Yet in a bid designed to arouse passions and jealousies, Debbie later found Craker and Scott with their arms around each other on the sofa. "All this was after you told Jayne you fancied Susan?" asked Richard Cherrill, defending. "Yes," replied Debbie. Then he added: "It was Jayne who brought

THE PASSIONATE AFFAIR SNOWBALLED... WITH DEBBIE SNEAKING HOME TO HER HUSBAND AFTER SEX SESSIONS WITH JAYNE

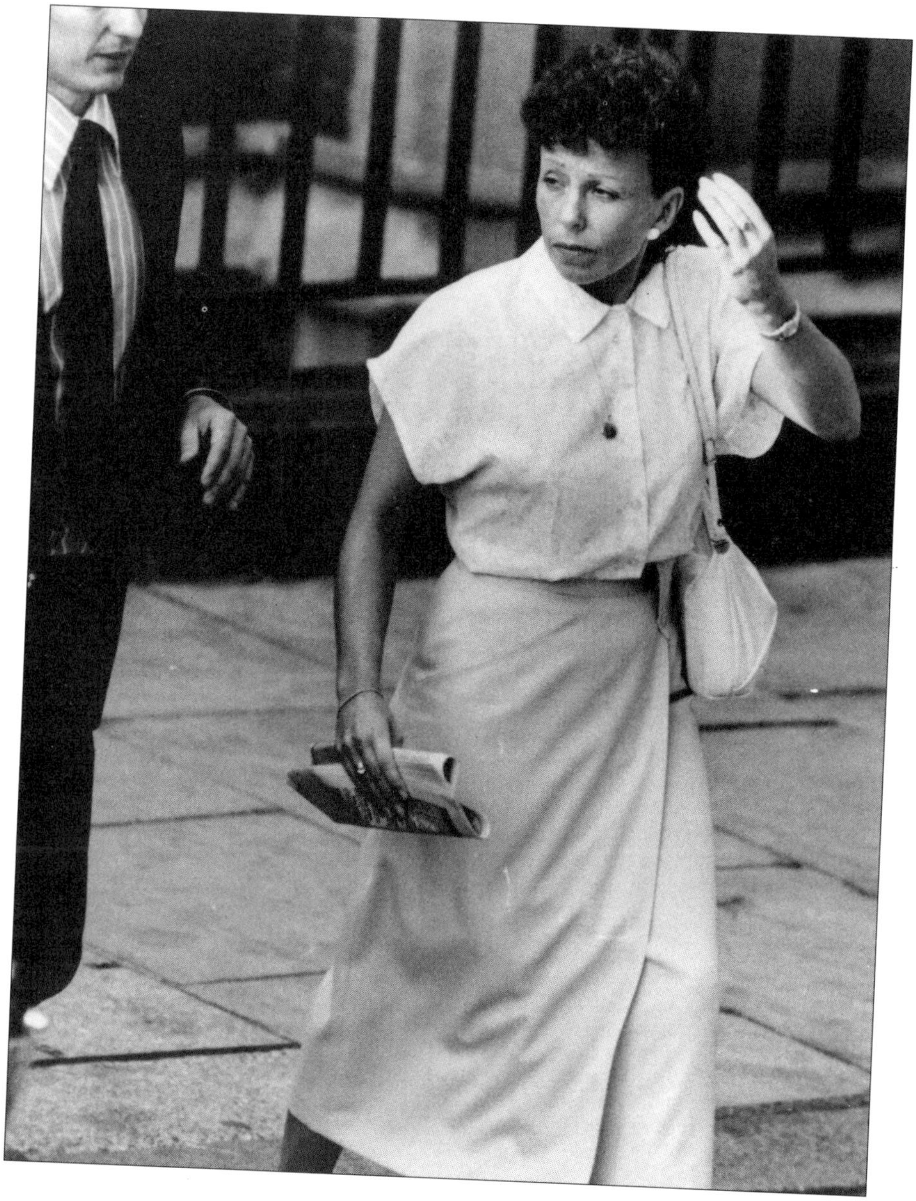

the sexual side of your relationship to an end by repulsing your advances, was it not?" Again she answered yes… which led events on to the 6 August 1985 when Susan Craker's dynamic world ended.

Above: ***Jayne Scott summons a taxi outside the Old Bailey after a trying day in the dock.***

Days before the attack Jayne Scott had gone to Sheffield to compete in a sporting tournament. During that weekend Debbie and Sue Craker shared an evening of lesbian sex. "We were in Susan's house on our own," Debbie told police. "During the evening we kissed each other several times. At some stage Sue said: 'Shall we go to bed?' I agreed. Sexual contact of a lesbian nature took place between us – Susan taking the dominant role." Such a one-night-stand could have been shared and kept secret forever – but Debbie confessed all to her lover. She said: "She was a very emotional person. There were tears, recriminations, sleepless nights and long silences." In the six days after Debbie had told of the amorous encounter Scott started demanding kisses and cuddles from Debbie, even though she had rejected her sexual advances for a period of more than a year. "She suddenly wanted more attention from me," said Debbie. "She wanted me to hold her or kiss her."

IN THE FRENZIED ATTACK, SUE CRAKER'S HEAD WAS, LITERALLY, BASHED IN WITH A CLAW HAMMER

She also wanted something much, much more, alleged the police. She wanted revenge against the deputy headmistress who claimed her "girl". Their case, denied by Scott, was that she went to Susan's home on August 6 1985 armed with a claw hammer. In an attack, the result of which police described as one of the most frenzied they had seen, Sue Craker's head was literally bashed in. Two gardeners working in the grounds of her home testified at Scott's trial how they heard eerie, moaning noises coming from inside the house… but thought it was someone "mucking around".

Gardener Ian Smith said: "It was like a moaning sound that went on for five minutes. We thought that someone was playing around and so we made the same noises back. Then it just stopped and there was silence." His workmate Nicholas Finney added: "We thought that it was someone having fun. We didn't think anyone was in pain. It was a sort of oohing noise, quite loud so as you could hear it over the noise of the lawnmowers."

A HORRIFYING SIGHT

Ian Scofield, Miss Craker's nephew who lived next door to her in Abbots Road, Barnet, said he rushed around to the house after the attack. He found his aunt wearing only a blouse and pants, groaning and gurgling on the floor amid a large pool of blood. Whatever the gardeners might have been able to do for her in terms of making her comfortable, the damage to her brain had already been completed with the first few blows of the hammer. Jayne Scott, despite her denials to police and to the court, had turned Miss Cracker into a vegetable.

The case was a sensation in Britain and involved hordes of journalists armed with fat chequebooks descending on Eton and Windsor seeking out the juicier background stories that would draw more and more people into the "secret lust of the netball

was not all that I thought it would be. I don't think it was normal for young people in their early twenties. We found our relationship was more like brother and sister than man and wife. I do not think that I got what I thought I would in marrying her. I did not get any early warning signs to tell me she might be lesbian. I think the split came because we had such a hectic social life and did such a lot of sport that we were apart too much. But I never thought of her being a lesbian. I was very young and I'm a lot older now and know a lot more and maybe now I would be able to pick signs out. When all this is

girls" inquiry. No-one was more surprised to find himself thrust into the limelight over the front-page case than Debbie Fox's ex-husband Stephen Fox. He had known nothing of his wife's lesbian affairs until he picked up his national newspaper one morning and read about her all over the front page. He said knowledge that he lost his wife to the charms of another woman hit him "like a bombshell", and that he was reeling from it days afterwards. Stephen, 28 at the time of the crime, had met Debbie when they worked together for an engineering firm in 1977.

They began dating and were married in the picture-postcard church of St. Giles in Stoke Poges in 1979. A financial accountant later in life, he said: "We were too young for marriage really. Gradually the marriage became like a brother and sister relationship. I remember that she was really nice looking. When you are that age you lust after everything in sight, but she was special. I had just broken up from a fairly long-standing relationship and Debbie was attractive, intelligent, quite a female altogether. But we just seemed to drift apart after we got married.

"I had no warning signs of Debbie's love for other women during the time we were together, three years in all. But my sex life

Above: ***Susan Craker is surrounded by Fleet Street pressmen after Scott is found guilty.***

Top: ***The Old Bailey, London, where Jayne Scott's frenzied attack was set out in gory detail.***

over I shall speak to her. I shall ask her why she did not tell me about what was coming up in court. All I knew was that she said there was a case coming up, but she didn't go into it."

Stephen split from Debbie in 1982 but they remained friends. Their divorce came around by mutual agreement on the grounds of separation – nothing to do with her extra marital affairs with other women. "I don't believe my wife had lesbian lovers

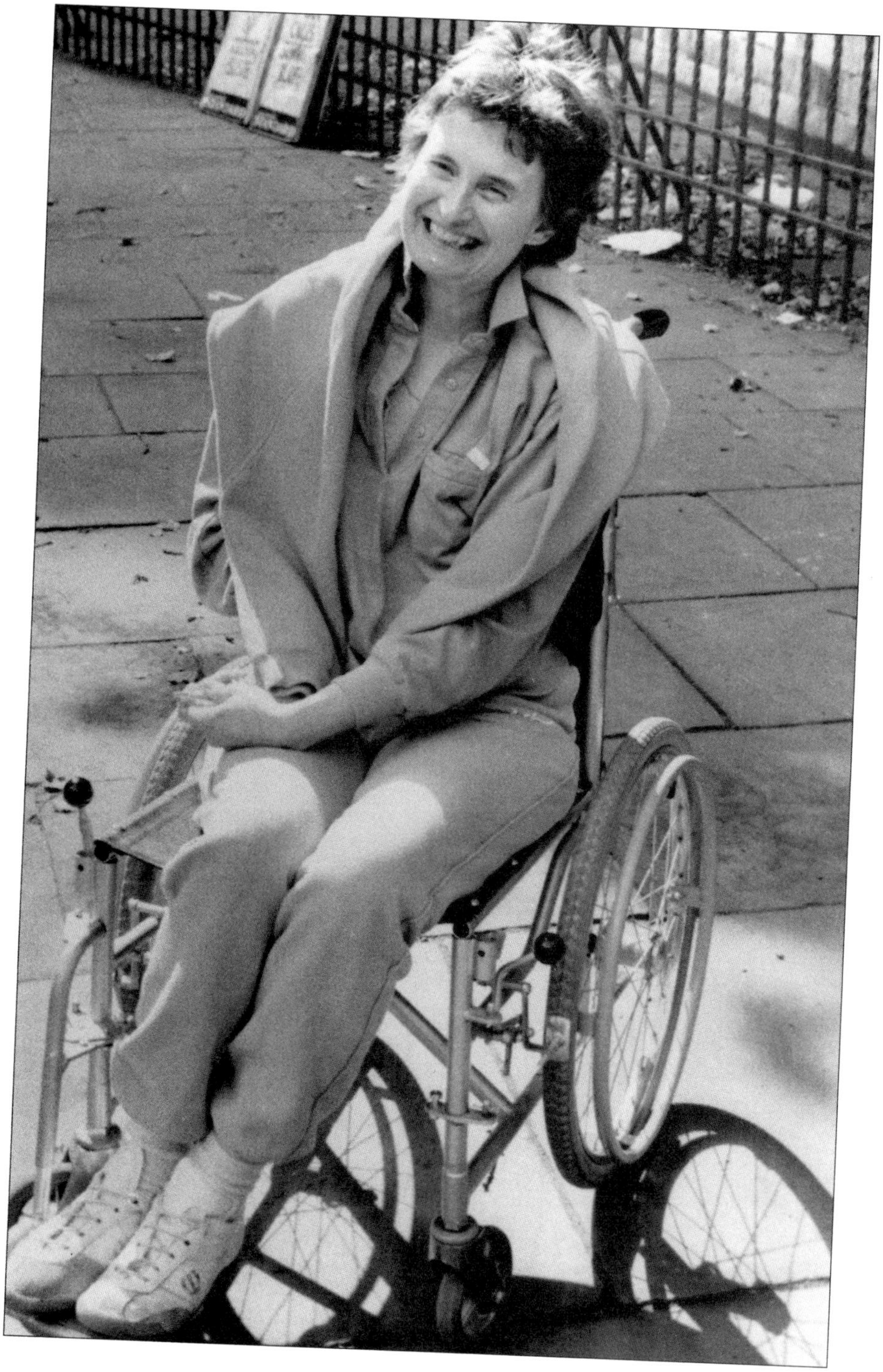

Above: ***The verdict was of some comfort for Miss Craker but nothing could give her back her previous life.***

while she was with me," he said. "I am planning to re-marry now and have told my fiancee all about Debbie. She understands that I now just have a friendly relationship with her and doesn't mind if I meet her and take her for a drink. This lesbian thing is quite staggering but it hasn't changed my opinion of Debbie."

Scott steadfastly maintained her innocence, hoping that a lack of forensic evidence tying her to the crime would make the police case come down to her word against theirs. But the circumstantial evidence against her piled up daily. Kate Potts took the stand to testify how she became a sort of go-between after Scott telephoned her to say that she suspected an affair between Fox and Craker.

Potts' relationship with Craker had fizzled in the weeks before the attack and she now lived alone. "I took the call on August 2, four days before the attack," said Potts. "She asked if she could see me to talk about Debbie and Sue. She just mentioned that she wanted to talk about their relationship. I did not know anything about the relationship. She seemed a bit fraught on the phone and I agreed she could come around about midday.

"When she arrived she was in control but very nervous, very on the edge. She said Debbie and Sue had been seeing each other in the previous week and would I find out what was going on. She said Debbie had stayed with Sue and had explained everything that happened.

"She said she went to see Sue the previous day to ask her to give up the relationship with Debbie. But Sue would not listen to her. I rang Sue while Scott was still in the house. I asked her what was happening and she said it was none of my business. She said she would not be intimidated. When I told Scott what Sue had just said to me it did not ease her at all. She said she and Debbie were going around to Sue's at the weekend and I thought it a very foolish idea and told her so."

A SOLID CONVICTION

The verdict when it came down was greeted with a look of shock and disbelief from the defendant. The jury of ten men and two women returned a unanimous verdict which proved beyond reasonable doubt that the woman from Farnham Royal, Berkshire, was guilty of the crime with which she was charged – grievous bodily harm with intent. Judge Michael Morland told her in the dock of victim Craker: "You all but destroyed her life." He rejected a plea from defence counsel Richard Cherrill for the sentence to be postponed so Scott could be considered for psychiatric treatment. He told her: "You have been convicted of an horrific crime. I accept that you were suffering from depression following your father's death. It's clear that you were

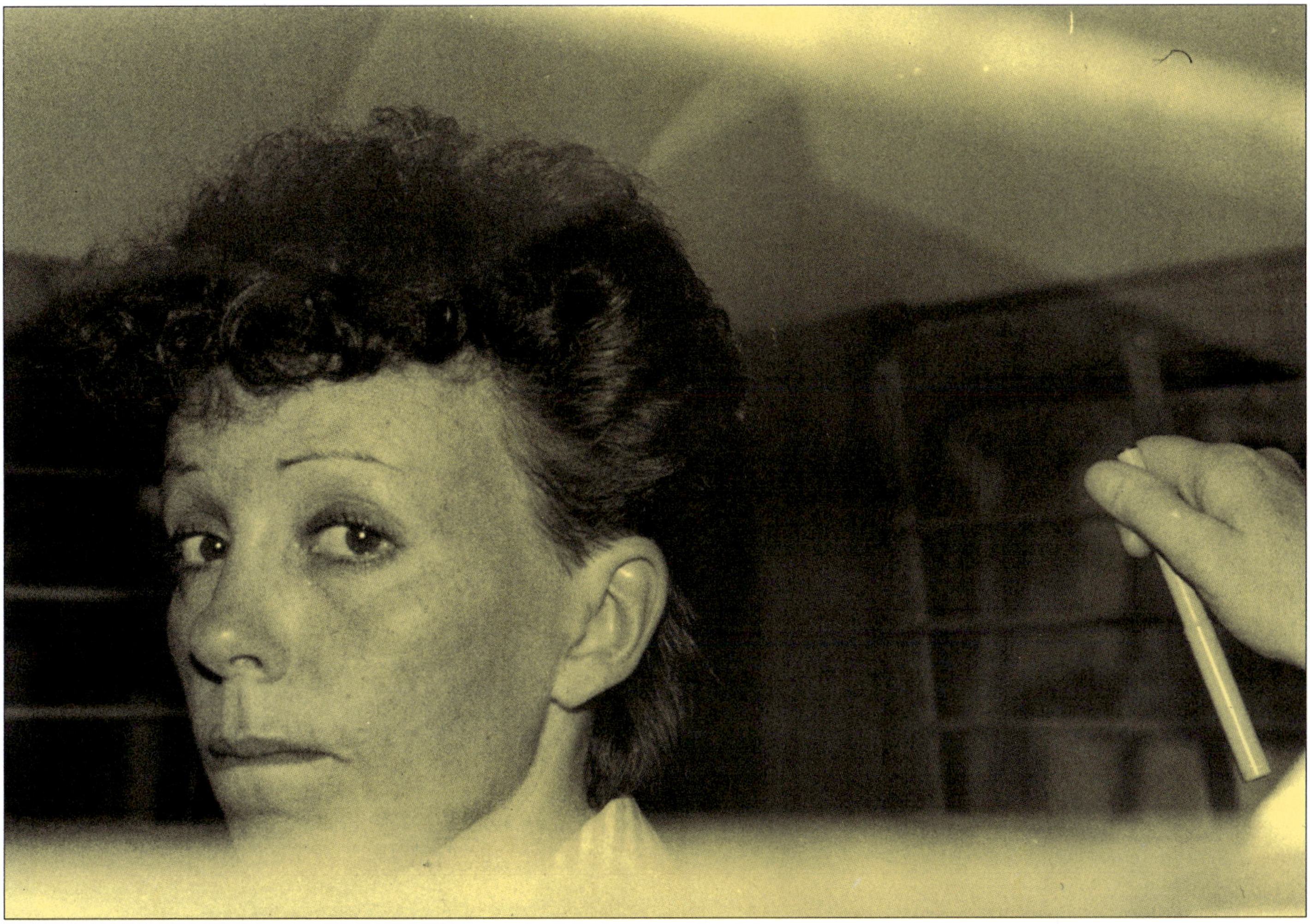

vulnerable to the burgeoning sexual relationship between Susan and Debbie. Your jealousy caused a loss of self control and you deliberately took the opportunity to bludgeon Sue Craker with the claw hammer, all but destroying her life." Scott went to the cells without a glance at the jury of her peers who had convicted her.

Outside the court there was solace in justice for Sue Craker – solace that could only be expressed in the staccato words she is now capable of due to her massive injuries. She told newsmen at the end of the two-week-long trial: "Thank God, thank God. Deserved everything she got... not enough... should be longer. Ruined my life... hope she suffers. Like me. Never forgive, never... Justice... done."

With the ending of the case came the inevitable "backgrounders" in the newspapers – the story-behind-the-story revelations that boosted sales in the sluggish summer months. Police officers involved in the case revealed that they were stunned by the extent of the lesbian network which spanned the playing fields and sports of the most English of areas.

One unamed officer said: "It was sex in the suburbs all right – only it was all women having it off with other women. It was quite an eye opener!" The police found a network spanning all walks of life and seemed astonished by it – yet those who had known Jayne Scott and the others said their lifestyle was merely one of those "open secrets" which so many know but say little about. Staff at the Monten Sports Centre in Slough, which had been used by the defendant for nine years, giggled behind her back at the passionate affairs that she pursued.

One 26-year-old woman attendant said: "Jayne was a very nice person – but everyone knew she was that way inclined. She wasn't the only one, though. Her sports attracted a lot of 'butch' girls and we knew there was a lot of hanky panky going on. One day the park-keeper opposite told us of a passionate lovemaking session he heard in the ladies' changing rooms!"

Above: ***Jayne Scott has one last glimpse of the world before she is taken away in a prison van to begin her sentence.***

"IT WAS SEX IN THE SUBURBS ALL RIGHT – ONLY IT WAS ALL WOMEN HAVING IT OFF WITH OTHER WOMEN"

"HER SPORTS ATTRACTED A LOT OF 'BUTCH' GIRLS AND WE KNEW THERE WAS A LOT OF HANKY PANKY GOING ON"

SOAP IN COURT
Taylforth's Big Blow

The Eastenders soap opera made a household name of Gillian Taylforth. But the flip side of fame brought misery to Gillian when her name appeared in a newspaper linked to a kinky sex act. She went to court to try to defeat the newspaper but ended up being humiliated and beaten in the courtroom.

Fighting a case for libel in the High Court in London can be like winning the pools... or losing at Russian roulette. For the aggrieved party who says his or her good name has been dragged through the mud in a publication there is the chance of great riches if the jury finds in their favour. Jeffrey Archer scooped £500,000 when a jury found he had been libelled by a newspaper which claimed he consorted with a prostitute. Elton John won a £1,000,000 settlement from The Sun newspaper which accepted there was no truth in its allegations that the singer had been with under-age rent boys. The paper caved in before the case was heard, mindful that legal bills – and a vengeful jury which always settles the sums to be paid – could have sent the final reckoning sky-high.

Yet for a person to lose can mean financial ruin. Sonia Sutcliffe, wife of the Yorkshire Ripper Peter Sutcliffe, was saddled with legal expenses close to £250,000

THERE IS THE CHANCE OF GREAT RICHES IF A HIGH COURT JURY FINDS IN FAVOUR OF A LIBELLED PARTY

Opposite: ***Gillian Taylforth enters the High Court with her boyfriend Geoff Knights.***

Below: ***Day in, day out, Gillian and Geoff Knights had to listen to damning testimony.***

Above: ***Gillian hoped that her reputation as a famous actress would rise above that of the often scurrilous Sun newspaper.***

THE SUN CLAIMED SHE HAD BEEN PERFORMING ORAL SEX ON KNIGHTS AS THEIR RANGE ROVER CAR WAS PARKED IN A LAY-BY

when she sued one newspaper too many after an incredible winning streak against the Fleet Street tabloids. It is a risk that is inherent when the action is brought because losing means paying one's own legal costs, plus the side of the defence. And when barristers of the A-Team of the legal profession are involved, such costs are significant. That is why most people mull over the pros and cons of launching a libel action carefully.

One can only assume that Gillian Taylforth, a leading actress in the BBC soap opera *Eastenders* had taken the best advice before deciding to take on The Sun in the High Court. But after a sensational trial which gripped the nation she ended up staring ruin in the face. She had pulled the trigger… and the chamber had been loaded. When the jurors returned to deliver their verdict after pondering on a case she felt certain of winning she suddenly found herself staring a £500,000 legal bill in the face. Not only that, but it was clear that a jury of her peers had found her guilty of performing a particularly lurid act – which she denied – and that it would go into the history books as fact.

Gillian Taylforth's ire was aroused by a story in The Sun newspaper which claimed she and her lover Geoff Knights had been caught by a police officer in a compromising position; that she was performing oral sex on him as their Range Rover car was parked in a lay-by off of the A1. The allegation was damaging enough to any person, irrespective of their standing in the community. But Miss Taylforth, as Kathy Beale in the super-popular TV series, had more to lose than most. Television is a fickle game and the image of an actress is everything. She is paid £80,000 a year for her role in the show which is watched by 19,000,000 people. This kind of publicity, she knew, was the kind that could destroy her acting career for good.

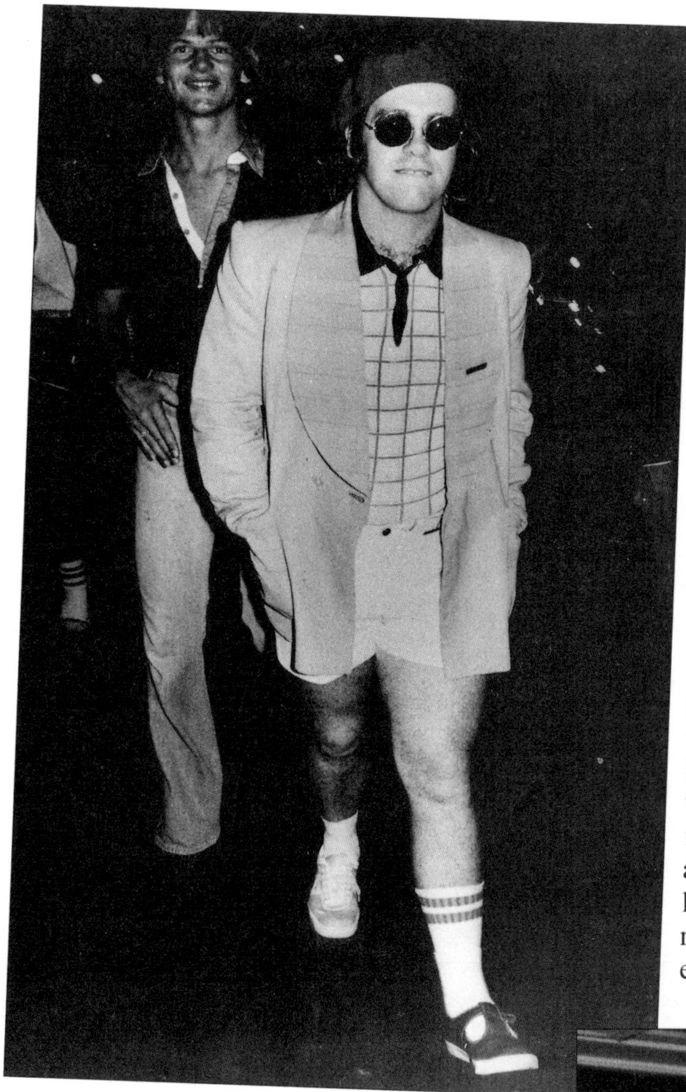

11 days and provide high theatre for Britain in the middle of a drab winter. There would be witnesses, explanations and a final, dramatic 11th hour video produced on behalf of The Sun which would finally clinch the case against her. Newspapers expended acres of space on it and it was the talking point of Britain. Clearly the cost for Ms. Taylforth in proceeding with it was not only financial – it also raked over a story that most people in the country, save those who read The Sun, had never heard of and gave it to an audience of tens of millions.

Court 13 was the setting for the drama in January 1994 and the principles played to the gallery with aplomb. Representing The Sun was George Carman, Q.C., the Torquemada of barristers, a man with a rapier sharp mind and an even sharper turn of phrase. He had gone to battle for and against newspapers in his time, but whoever he was representing had

THE CASE RAKED OVER A STORY THAT MOST PEOPLE IN THE COUNTRY HAD NEVER HEARD OF AND GAVE IT TO MILLIONS

Left: ***Elton John took £1,000,000 from The Sun over allegations that he had sex with under-age rent boys.***

Below: ***Lord Jeffrey Archer with wife Mary. He too went to battle in the High Court to clear his name and won record damages. Gillian Taylforth would not be so lucky.***

The story first appeared in 1992 in The Sun. The implication was that the couple were having oral sex when a police officer chanced upon the vehicle parked in a slip-road off of the A1 at Borehamwood, Herts. It quoted police as saying Knights had been cautioned for an indecent act. The story from Miss Taylforth was simply that she had been leaning over to rub his stomach because he had drunk too much champagne at Royal Ascot and was feeling queasy.

A BIG GAMBLE

It was left to a jury of four women and eight men to prove, beyond reasonable doubt, who was telling the truth. If it was 38-year-old Miss Taylforth she stood to gain a massive amount of money and all legal costs would have to be picked up by The Sun. But a loss could prove catastrophic – yet it was a risk she was willing to take "for my good name". The trial was to last

Above: ***Gillian Taylforth with friend Steve McFadden before the verdict that wiped the smile from her face.***

bought the best. Peter Carter-Ruck, himself one of the top libel lawyers in Britain, said: "He is the first choice in any criminal case and certainly one of the leading choices in libel cases. He is extremely thorough in the preparation of his cases and even in cross-examination can get pretty near offensive." Yet no-one ever accused a court of law as being a finishing school for girls – and Miss Taylforth was to find out for herself just how brutal George Carman could be as he hacked away for the truth.

Her evidence was simple: that Knights had suffered a "pancreatic attack" after drinking the champagne and that she was rubbing his stomach to soothe away the pain. "How could anyone think I would stop on the A1 to have oral sex?" she asked the court quizzically.

"It was cheap and really made me feel sick to my stomach." Her QC Michael Beloff, whose fees would eventually top out at around £75,000, tried to suggest that the policeman whose unhappy lot it was to stumble across the couple, was doing it for some kind of glory, of making the story up "and revelling in the limelight".

MISS TAYLFORTH WAS TO FIND JUST HOW BRUTAL GEORGE CARMAN COULD BE AS HE HACKED AWAY FOR THE TRUTH

But P.C. Terry Talbot was a man whose evidence was firm and measured in every way. He told the court that he had approached the parked car and saw Taylforth's head "moving slowly up and down" over her lover's lap. He also said he saw Mr. Knight's exposed manhood. Under increased pressure that he was somehow mistaken or otherwise disposed to give inaccurate testimony, the 49-year-old officer said: "If I stood here until Christmas I would not change anything I said or saw."

Indeed, he said he had in fact been too soft on the soap star and should have arrested her and Knights instead of merely cautioning them. That was backed up by his superior, Inspector Francis Monoghan, who said: "The actress should have been arrested along with Mr. Knights for outraging public decency and using abusive language." It was clearly quite a strain on the copper who had twice been commended for bravery in the line of duty. PC Derek Sweeny, a colleaugue, said after the case: "It was such a terrible thing hanging over him that he was mentally breaking up. He is a very well-thought-of officer and everyone was behind him. Everyone knew he would tell nothing but the truth."

Bringing the case to court also exposed practically every other facet of their lives, including Taylforth's relationship with Knights, a man for whom the term "flash" seems to have been invented. The Daily Mail newspaper went so far as to state: "Knights could have stepped straight from the streets of Walford, fictional home of BBC TV's *Eastenders*. A strapping playboy wheeler-dealer, he has dated a series of page three girls, has a taste for flash cars and has a number of convictions for burglary, criminal damage and assault."

A BAD HISTORY

Indeed, the litany of his run-ins with the law were seen by libel experts as seriously damaging the couple's standing in the eyes of the jury. Far from seeming a couple with reputations to lose, they began to be perceived as a couple yet to get them. "They became objects of ridicule," said The Guardian. "The jury appeared to be enraptured as the courtroom scenes ranged from moments of humour and emotion to outright sleaze."

The year before the case Knights had punched an *Eastenders* scriptwriter in a brawl after he had claimed an affair with her. The trial for him seemed embarrassing more than anything – especially when it came to a piece of police evidence which he clearly had not remembered anything about.

On the night that P.C. Talbot had interrupted his "stomach rub" he had signed a police caution admitting the sexual offence. The only defence he had for that was that he had drunk a lot of champagne and didn't know what he was signing. He did not seem to enjoy the police version of events which had him outside Borehamwood police station – Miss Taylforth had been allowed to drive home to look after their baby daughter Jessica – where it was alleged he said: "Take your uniforms off and I will fight you outside." The police

IT WAS ALLEGED THAT KNIGHTS HAD SAID TO POLICE: "TAKE YOUR UNIFORMS OFF AND I WILL FIGHT YOU OUTSIDE"

said Knights calmed down and agreed to a caution over the sex act with the words: "You know how it is – we had a good day at the races and just got carried away!" He denied it, but the theatre surrounding the case was escalating daily.

The case was proving hilarious for those not directly involved in it. Long a nation used to the nudge-nudge, wink-wink humour of Benny Hill, many newspapers began running daily joke columns, each one playing off the blue humour of the court case. Comedians like Bernard Manning, known for his coarser-than-coarse jokes, said: "Gillian Taylforth asked this scouser if he wanted a blow job and he replied: 'Not if it affects my Giro cheque!'" The Daily Star – a newspaper which forked out £500,000 to Jeffrey Archer six years earlier, ran a Blue Jokes on Gillian half-page which included: "What's the difference between a willy and a German sausage? No? Well, let's go for a picnic!" The jokes were mildly amusing and lapped up by an audience that craved more and

Below: ***Gillian in her*** **Eastenders** ***role with Albert Square market trader Pete Beale.***

GILLIAN CONFESSED TO FRIENDS HALFWAY THROUGH THE TRIAL THAT SHE WISHED SHE HAD NEVER BROUGHT IT

Right: ***A videotape of Gillian performing an obscene act on a bottle for a joke at a party was to prove crucial in her losing the case.***

Below: ***Geoff Knights and Gillian enjoying happier times, in the Range Rover where the sex act was alleged to have taken place.***

more details of the actress and her "past". But it was no laughing matter for Gillian who confessed to friends midway through the trial that she wished that she had never brought the matter to court.

Perhaps the most hilarious moment occurred when the judge Mr. Justice Drake agreed to a reconstruction of the incident in the car park of the High Court! Miss Taylforth and Knights were in the vehicle to depict themselves on the night in question while a couple of Sun reporters acted out P.C. Talbot's version of events. The Sun then pictured another reconstruction in their newspages the following day. It seemed as if there was no sanctuary left in England from the all-embracing courtcase.

But if the reconstruction was mildly amusing to all involved, the same cannot be said of the trump card of the defence, a video tape which the defence tried in two hours of legal argument to block. Miss Taylforth clearly had no idea what the video contained when the judge consented to let it be screened and High Court staff moved into Court 13 to fix up the necessary screens and apparatus. It was later learned that the video was taken by a man known as "Herbie". Herbie had called The Sun at the 11th hour claiming that the video would vindicate the newspaper entirely. The Sun claimed that two unidentified men later handed the video over, no money changed hands and the judge was satisfied that "nothing improper" had occurred in getting the video. It clinched the case for The Sun.

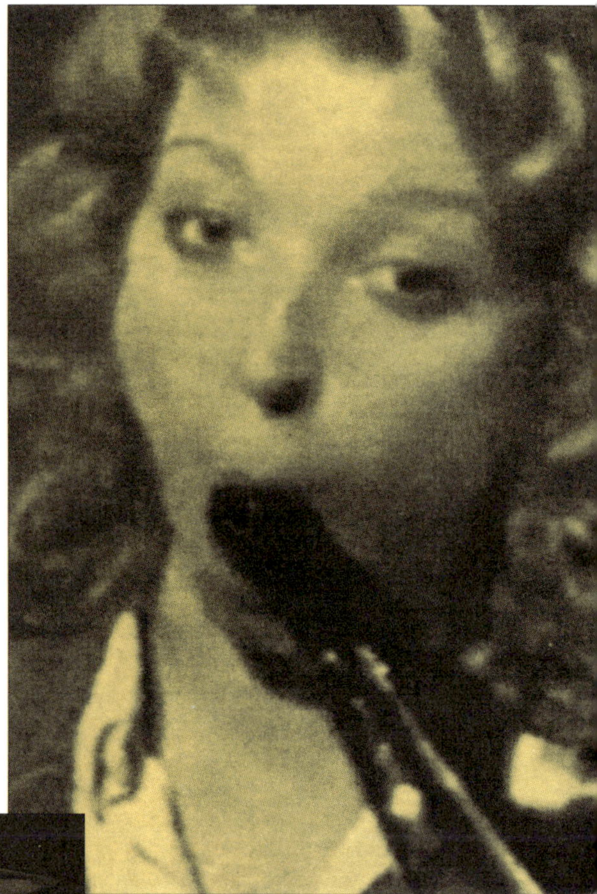

You could have heard a pin drop in the court as the tape was played. It destroyed Taylforth's carefully cultivated image of a woman wronged by both the police and a press report. The video showed her simulating oral sex at a party with a wine bottle and a large German sausage and above the lurid images could be heard her words: "I'd like to state I give good head. I give very good head."

The video was made during a lunchtime party with some showbiz friends at a small theatre in North London. It was a private affair and it would have remained so forever had Gillian Taylforth not chosen to take the newspaper to court. Now the video which she said was "a joke" was being used to damn her. George Carman went in for the kill: "The tacky and cheap video exposed her performance in the wit-

THE TAPE DESTROYED HER CAREFULLY CULTIVATED IMAGE OF A WOMAN WRONGED BY THE POLICE AND A PRESS REPORT ness box as a sham. She is not quite the demure lady.

"Miss Taylforth's daughter Jessica has been waved in and out of the script as if she is the president of the Mother's Union. That is not the whole picture. The reality is that there is another side that has been carefully concealed from you. It is not a shameful side. It is a coarser side. Drunk or otherwise, with friends or otherwise, Gillian Taylforth was behaving in a way that one hopes the majority of women in this country would never behave. And she was doing that because in drink she can be given to a certain coarseness in sexual matters. Of course that doesn't prove she was having oral sex in a car. The words 'I give good head' could be her epitaph." Carman, nicknamed the Silver Fox within the rarified atmosphere of the law courts, had been at his best… or worst.

A SAD FIGURE

It took over five hours for the jury to retire and reach their verdict. When they came back into court Taylforth seemed to crumble when they took their places. Her fingers clutched at a silver charm and the jury avoided her eyes. The foreman stood and said that a majority verdict had been reached. When he said it was for the defendants – The Sun – there was a moan from Miss Taylforth as her sister Janice hissed at a police sergeant who had given evidence: "Satisfied, are you?" Outside the court as the legal minutiae was tied up – namely that Taylforth and Knights were responsible for the estimated £500,000 legal bill – she collapsed and needed to be taken to St. Bartholomew's Hospital by ambulance.

Later, putting a stoical face on a disastrous end to a disastrous case, she said: "I am emotionally drained. If I had known then what I know now I don't think I could have gone through the ordeal of the case. But at the end of the day it is all about clearing your name and that is what Geoff and I tried to do. I was in deep shock when the verdict came in – I just couldn't breathe. Finding the money to pay these costs will be a serious struggle. It's not going to be easy. My whole character has changed. My faith in human nature has gone. I have come out of this a very, very cynical person. I have always been an open and honest person – but I know now that I have come out of this a different woman. The video was a joke, taken by someone who was a friend from the age of 17. Someone I trusted. I don't know who gave or sold that video. I feel I cannot trust anybody now."

Susan Aslan, a libel lawyer at a London law firm, said: "This has hammered home the point that libels are always risky, when it is one person's word against another. It is like playing Russian Roulette with the jury. There is never more than a 50-50 chance in most cases. I spend a lot of time talking people out of bringing such proceedings." Gillian Taylforth, of *Eastenders* fame, had spun the barrel on the gun… and lost.

"GILLIAN TAYLFORTH WAS BEHAVING IN A WAY THAT ONE HOPES THE MAJORITY OF WOMEN WOULD NEVER BEHAVE"

Below: ***Gillian Taylforth leaves hospital accompanied by Knights. She had collapsed at the end of the libel trial that she had lost.***

A BLOODY END
The Death of Dillinger

John Dillinger was a criminal who lived by the gun and eventually died by it. There was no trial for Dillinger, no fancy lawyers to argue that he was the victim of society. He got his comeuppance the way that most said he deserved – violently, shot down after an elaborate FBI plan had come to fruition.

John Dillinger scorched his mark on the depression years in America like a branding iron. He was the most famous and most ruthless desperado of all. So daring were his actions and so successful his evasion of the full might of American crimefighters that laws were passed in Congress to find new ways to end his crime spree. He was rotten to the core, but to the forces of law and order he was becoming that most dangerous type of criminal – a hero to the man in the street.

These were hard times and even though he had murdered wantonly in his escapades and people viewed anyone who was getting their own back at a system which had deserted them as a Robin Hood figure.

Yet this Robin Hood gave nothing away – everything was done for the greater glory and greed of John Dillinger himself and no-one else. When he eventually died in spectacular fashion, outside a movie theatre in Chicago, America's attorney general of the

HE WAS BECOMING THAT MOST DANGEROUS TYPE OF CRIMINAL – A FOLK HERO TO THE MAN IN THE STREET

Opposite: ***John Dillinger, Public Enemy No. 1.***

Below: ***John Dillinger, in the white shirt second from right, after his 1934 capture.***

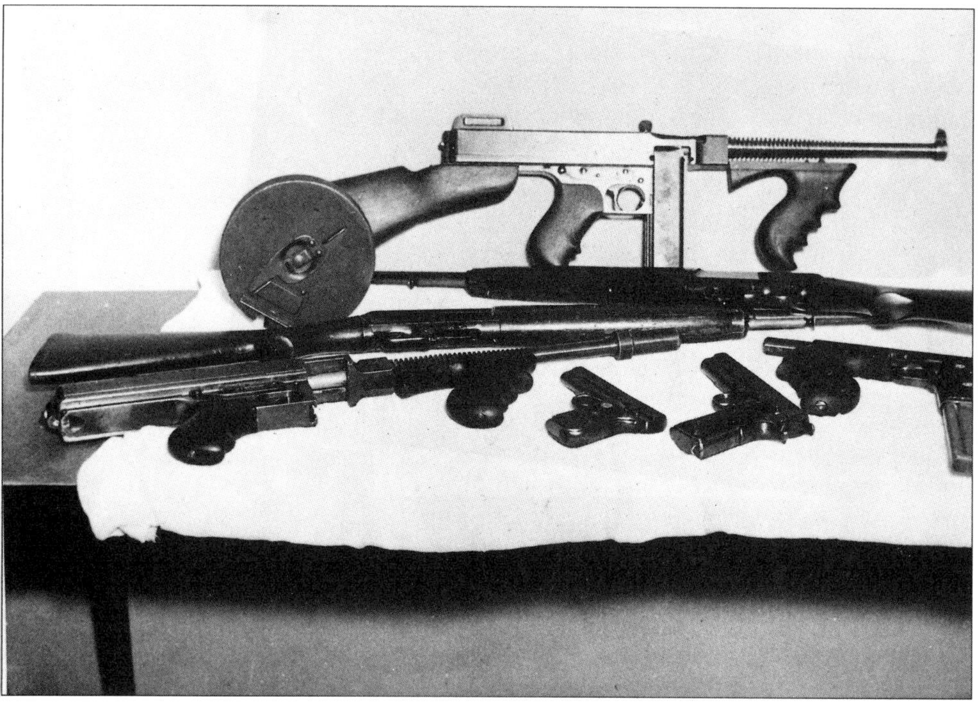

Above: ***The tools of his murderous trade – weapons used by John Dillinger during his crime career.***

times was moved to say: "I find his death gratifying. It has saved the taxpayer a lot of money in a trial, for there can be no question that he would have lied to the end."

The man who would rise to the top of the FBI's most wanted list to become Public Enemy No.1 began his criminal career in 1920, even though his most hair–raising exploits were all carried out in a remarkably short period of time in the early 1930s. John Toland, whose 1963 biography of the outlaw is regarded as one of the definitive works on his crime career, said: "John Dillinger, in the opinion of many, is the greatest folk hero of American crime. He was never mixed up with the vice or gambling rackets. He never tortured or shot his accomplices.

"Working with only a friend, or a small group, he was essentially a loner, an operator who planned and executed daring bank robberies and prison escapes. He came from a modest, rural, midwest background but somehow seemed destined to act out his role in the large cities. The banks that he knocked off were countless and Billy the Kid's exploits today seem child's play in comparison."

A BRUTAL YOUTH

Born in 1902 in Indianapolis, he was marked down as a bad seed by his teachers in school. Shrewd and cunning, ruthless and self centred, one master remarked that he had all the attributes for a career in

Right: ***President Franklyn Roosevelt signs a tough anti-crime bill aimed at curbing the exploits of Dillinger and his kind. Directly behind him is J. Edgar Hoover, the FBI director who swore to get Dillinger one way or the other.***

crime – which is exactly what he was planning. Dillinger Jnr. burned with all the indignation of his countrymen who grew up poor with little government help. Life was a black and white affair to him – those who had and those who had not. He was most definitely in the latter, but his unique skills would place him in the former. Crime started off as juvenile burglaries and car thefts before he began to home in on those repositories of wealth – the banks. He had briefly held a job in a machine shop when he was 17, but the only items he seemed to fashion on the shop's lathe were replica guns – a skill that would one day stand him in good stead.

In September 1924 he was already on the run for having deserted the Navy after five months' service. With an accomplice he attempted to rob a grocery store in the

small town of Mooresville, where he had moved four years previously. But the store owner, Bertram Morgan, had an alarm wired up to the local police station, a novel device in those days. Soon cops were swarming all over the store and Dillinger was arrested without a shot being fired. He and his companion were sentenced to serve between ten and 21 years in jail, their term to be determined by their behaviour inside the penitentiary. He twice tried to escape but in 1933, as the nation suffered like a prisoner upon the rack from the ravages of the Great Depression, the state governor took pity upon him and he was granted a pardon. It would go down as one of the great misguided judgements of all time.

A BAD TRAVELLER

Within less than a month he had procured firearms from the Chicago underworld and embarked on his legendary crime spree. With a moll at his side he first hit the payroll of a thread-making factory in Monticello, Illinois. Then in July 1933 he took $3,000 in an armed raid at a bank in Montpelier, Indiana. Raids in Daleville, Ohio and Indianapolis followed, each one more daring than the last. In the Indianapolis raid he was seemingly cornered – but some sixth sense told him to bolt for the rear of the building where he found a door unlocked. He walked calmly into the street and mingled with the lunchtime crowds – with the $28,000 in stolen loot still with him.

Above: ***The Depression bred the conditions of hopelessness which turned Dillinger into a folk hero in the eyes of many.***

Left: ***To the man in the street without a penny, the idea of Dillinger robbing the rich man's banks made him into a Robin Hood type of figure.***

HE WALKED CALMLY INTO THE STREET AND MINGLED WITH THE CROWDS – WITH THE STOLEN LOOT STILL WITH HIM

dollar robbery at the First National Bank in Chicago. It was a murder which shocked America and placed him at the top of the FBI most wanted list.

For three months Dillinger laid low, undergoing rudimentary plastic surgery to change his appearance. His chin was altered to disguise a tell-tale cleft in his chin, a mole on his face had been removed and there had been crude acid-burns applied to his fingertips in a bid to remove the prints. Experts said these would have caused him excruciating pain when done – and for nothing, as it turned out, because upon death his fingerprints were as crystal clear as the day he was born.

Soon it was time for him to go hunting again and he chose a bank in Tucson, Arizona – way out west and far from his usual stomping grounds around America's heartland. But this time it went badly wrong. Heavy bank security and police back-up surrounded him and his cohorts within minutes. There were no shots fired as Dillinger was led away in chains to await his destiny with the electric chair. But, after having been transferred back to Indiana, where most of his crimes had been committed, he staged the kind of spectacular escape that set polite society in Paris, Rome, Berlin and London talking about his exploits as well as all of America.

Above: ***Dillinger affects a pose of supreme disinterest during one of the many court appearances he made during his violent life.***

After the Indianapolis raid he was caught three days later, on September 25, in Dayton, Ohio, and sent to jail in Lima, Ohio, to await the arrival of an FBI investigating team. But members of his gang broke into the jail and murdered sheriff Jessee Sarber to spring him. Dillinger took a shot at the sheriff too. Dillinger now had blood on his hands and knew that there was no looking back.

Any capture in any state would mean extradition to the state where the most serious crime occurred – and ultimately a date with the electric chair. Instead of going underground with his not-inconsiderable reserves of loot he opted instead to increase the tempo of his activities. Raid followed raid – one on a police armoury to steal bullet proof jackets and machine guns, one on a bank that netted $144,000, another bank raid, this time in Wisconsin, where he stole $28,000, and a raid in Chicago. On January 15 1934 in Chicago he shot and killed Patrolman Patrick O'Malley in a $20,000

ANY CAPTURE IN THE STATE WOULD MEAN EXTRADITION AND, ULTIMATELY, A DATE WITH THE ELECTRIC CHAIR

DEADLY SKILLS

Remembering his skill learned from the short time spent in the machine shop as a youth he fashioned an authentic-looking gun from wood in the prison workshop. Using some black boot polish he gave the gun a metallic hue. Using this he held up a guard, marched out into the street and was gone! His fame was never higher… the frustration of the authorities to hold down this Houdini of hold-ups never greater. The escape cemented his Robin Hood image in another way. He took two hostages out of the prison gates with him and gave each of them $4 for their cab fare home! This was big money during the Great Depression and was the kind of PR that the forces of law and order despised.

"Events followed swiftly after that," the New York Times wrote breathlessly of his exploits. "They multiplied until his name became a byword for outlawry, his existence a political shibboleth, his career a reason for the passing of laws in congress and the posting of rewards. Spectacular in the way he staged his lawless escapades, devil-may-care in his encounters with the law, he nevertheless brought every possible modern facility into play in his skirmishes. He used fast cars. He had bullet proof vests. His men used machine guns."

Although just two deaths were directly attributed to Dillinger, there had in fact been 16 lawmen killed by his gang members in shootouts and escapes. The law of "common purpose" applied across America and John Dillinger was jointly held responsible for them all.

"HE BROUGHT EVERY MODERN FACILITY INTO PLAY IN HIS SKIRMISHES... FAST CARS... BULLET PROOF VESTS... MACHINE GUNS"

In April 1934 he and the gang decided to rest up again in woods in Little Bohemia, Wisconsin. There, amid respectable holidaymakers, the hoods rented a cabin and spent time sunbathing, fishing and playing endless games of cards. But the underworld was talking now and a massive armed task force of agents descended on the quiet wooded area for what they hoped would be the final showdown with Dillinger and his boys. On April 22 there were terrifying gun battles raging all day in the woods. Two lawmen were killed and several of Dillinger's men wounded, but the arch criminal and several others escaped in cars. He had eluded the law once more but he knew that the trap had been sprung due to the lure of the $15,000 reward. The government knew it too and consequently upped the money to $25,000 – around £150,000 by today's standards.

Dillinger decided to retire to Chicago after putting around rumours that he had been killed in the running gun battles in

Below: ***Chicago, the Windy City, became a playground for such gangsters as Al Capone and John Dillinger.***

Above: ***The Biograph Cinema on the night John Dillinger was gunned down outside it.***

Right: ***The girl whose photo was in John Dillinger's watch: Polly Hamilton.***

DILLINGER LIVED LIKE A PRIVATE, LAW-ABIDING CITIZEN FOR THE FIRST TIME SINCE HE WAS A SCHOOLBOY

Wisconsin. He took the name Jimmie Lawrence, a board of trade clerk, and began seeing an attractive 26-year-old divorced waitress called Polly Hamilton. Polly was hooked on the dashing good looks and casual manner of the man she knew as Jimmie – even more hooked when he bought her a diamond ring and gave her $50 for a visit to the dentist. Polly rented a room from a friend called Anna Sage, a woman who had twice been convicted and pardoned of running a brothel. She had been busted a third time and on this occasion there was to be no let-off; when John Dillinger moved under her roof she was staring at deportation to her native Romania, a prospect she truly dreaded.

In this period Dillinger lived like a private, law-abiding citizen for the first time since he was a schoolboy. He knew the great manhunt was still on, but he severed his contact with underworld pals and kept a low profile. He enjoyed leisurely meals, movies in air-conditioned cinemas and going to nightclubs with Polly. He was pondering a move to Mexico and made tentative arrangements to fly there on the morning of July 23, unaware that he would be dead 24 hours before departure time, the pieces of silver on his head too tempting for someone to resist.

A SERIOUS MANHUNT

FBI Director J. Edgar Hoover had sent special agent Sam Cowley to Chicago after receiving information that he had fled there. Hoover said to him: "Stay on Dillinger. Go everywhere the trail takes you. Take everyone who was ever remotely connected to the gang. Take him alive if you can but protect yourself." But a situation that had no connection to the FBI or the chase was about to bring the case of Public Enemy No.1 to its climax.

Anna Sage, the woman who was facing deportation, had learned through her own contacts in the criminal fraternity who the board of trade clerk living with Polly really was. She was not only tempted by the large reward – she was tempted by the possibility of cutting a deal with the immigration authorities intent on deporting her from

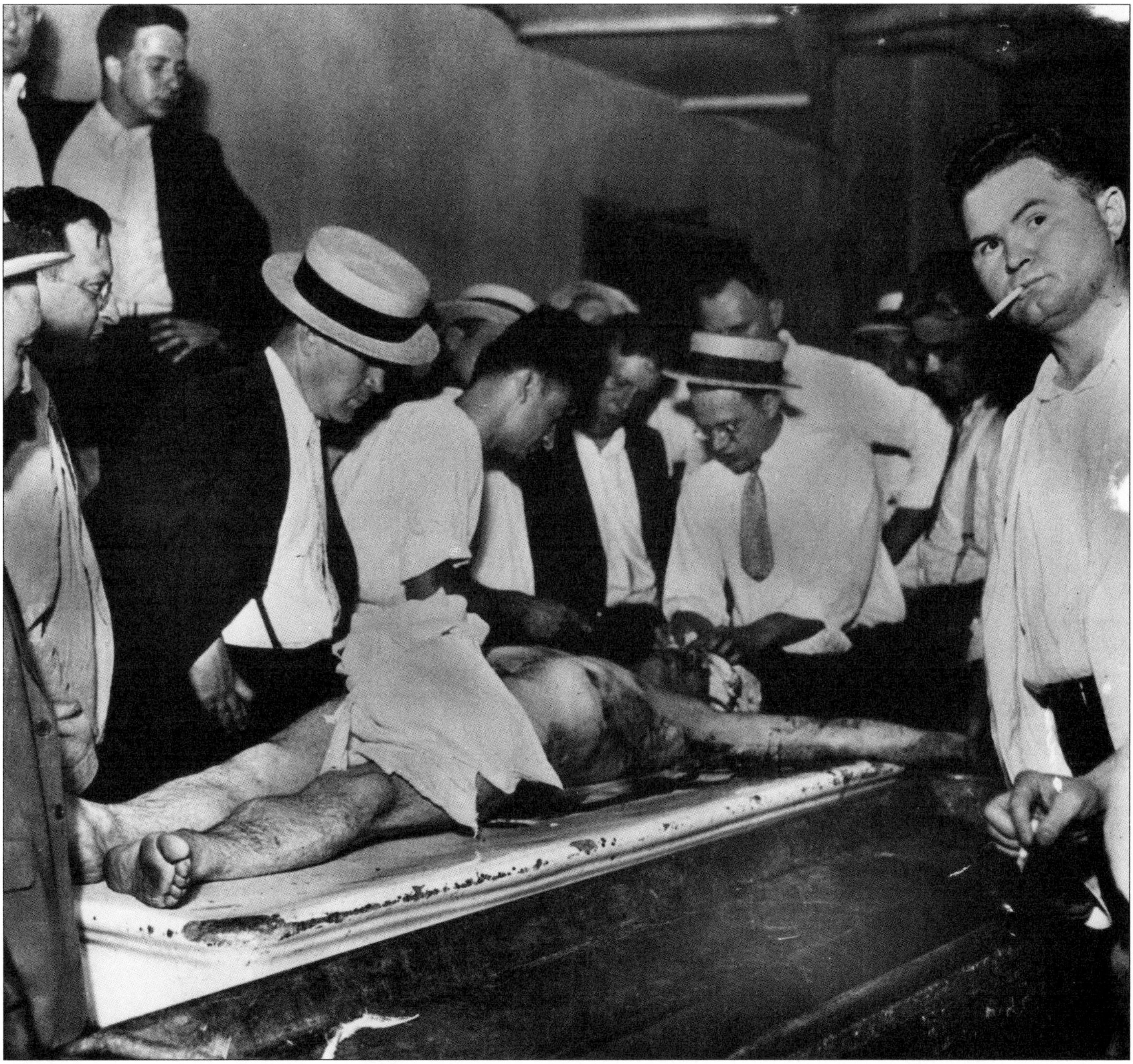

Above: ***The bullet-ridden body of John Dillinger is examined by lawmen and the plain curious at the local morgue after he was gunned down.***

America . After negotiating with policemen whom she knew she was finally granted an audience with senior officers at a secret meeting on the shore of Lake Michigan late at night. Satisfied that the lawmen would both pay her the reward money and use their clout to stop her being deported, she ratted on the gangster.

Sunday July 22 was a hot and muggy day in Chicago, so hot that 23 people would die from weather-related problems. The cinemas were a favourite spot in the city because of their air conditioning. Sage had told the police that Dillinger and Polly were planning a trip to the Marbro movie theatre. Or possibly the Biograph. At 7.00pm Sage telephoned the FBI to say: "He's here. He's just come. I am going with them. Probably the Marbro or the Biograph. I don't know." She hung up, leaving the agents scrambling to cover both theatres. Special agents trained in marksmanship covered both of them, all entrances and exits. They wanted him alive, but if there was trouble he would be gunned down like a dog. The case had a unique aspect to it already – so keen were the FBI on maintaining security that they didn't even tell the Chicago police of the operation they were mounting.

But the presence outside the cinema of so many plainclothes men aroused the suspicion of the manager, fearful that he was to become the victim of another box-office hold up. He telephoned the police, who arrived just as Dillinger was exiting the Biograph at 10.30pm, having watched *Manhattan Melodrama* starring Clark Gable and William Powell. The picture ended with the villain, Gable, walking to the electric chair.

ANIMAL CUNNING

Dillinger's feral senses stirred as he saw men flashing identification badges to other men outside the theatre and his hand reached inside his jacket pocket for the loaded Colt automatic nestling there. He knew something was up and knew that he could only bolt for it. In a low crouch he ran into the alley at the side of the cinema. The gun was in his hand now and before he had gone 20 paces the barked commands to halt were being shouted ater him.

Two agents opened fire on him, one bullet hitting his left side, the other tearing into his back and exiting through his right eye. He was stone dead before he hit the hot cobblestones.

Dillinger died a few blocks from the garage where the Al Capone gang had wiped out rivals in the infamous St. Valentine's Day Massacre. As agents went into the Biograph to telephone Hoover in Washington with the good news, Dillinger's body was taken to the Cook County Morgue for an autopsy.

It was there that the extent of his plastic surgery became clear – and also how ineffective his fingerprint mutilation had been. The acid had failed to do its work and the whorls of all his dabs came out crystal clear; it was the concrete identification the FBI needed that they had their man. A few minutes after he had been deposited at the morgue Sgt. Frank Reynolds of the Dillinger squad – a man who had spent two years hunting him – came in. He was so glad to see his nemesis dead that he shook the hand of the corpse. Meanwhile, outside

Above and Right: ***Before and after. His death mask after he was shot and how he looked before he paid for plastic surgery with the loot from his bank raids.***

ONE BULLET HIT HIM ON HIS LEFT SIDE, THE OTHER TORE INTO HIS BACK AND EXITED THROUGH HIS RIGHT EYE

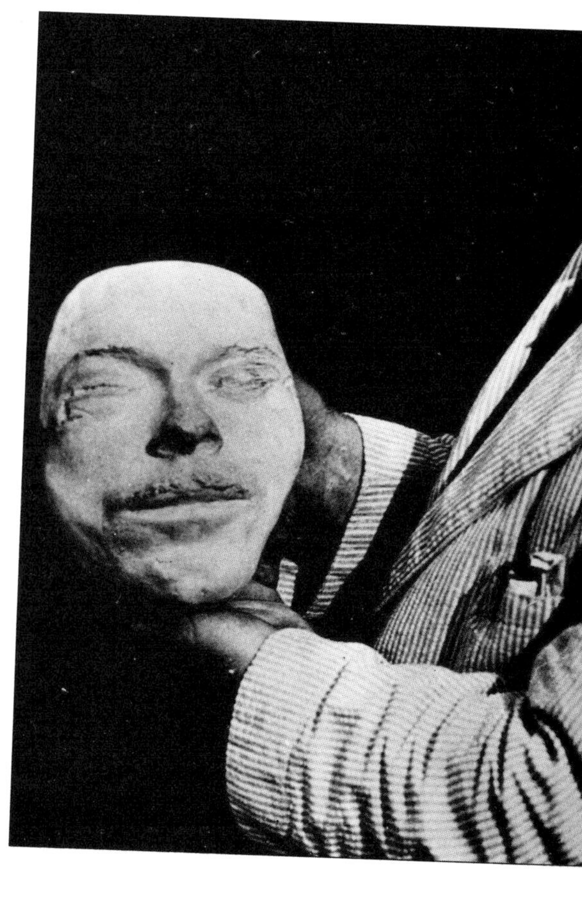

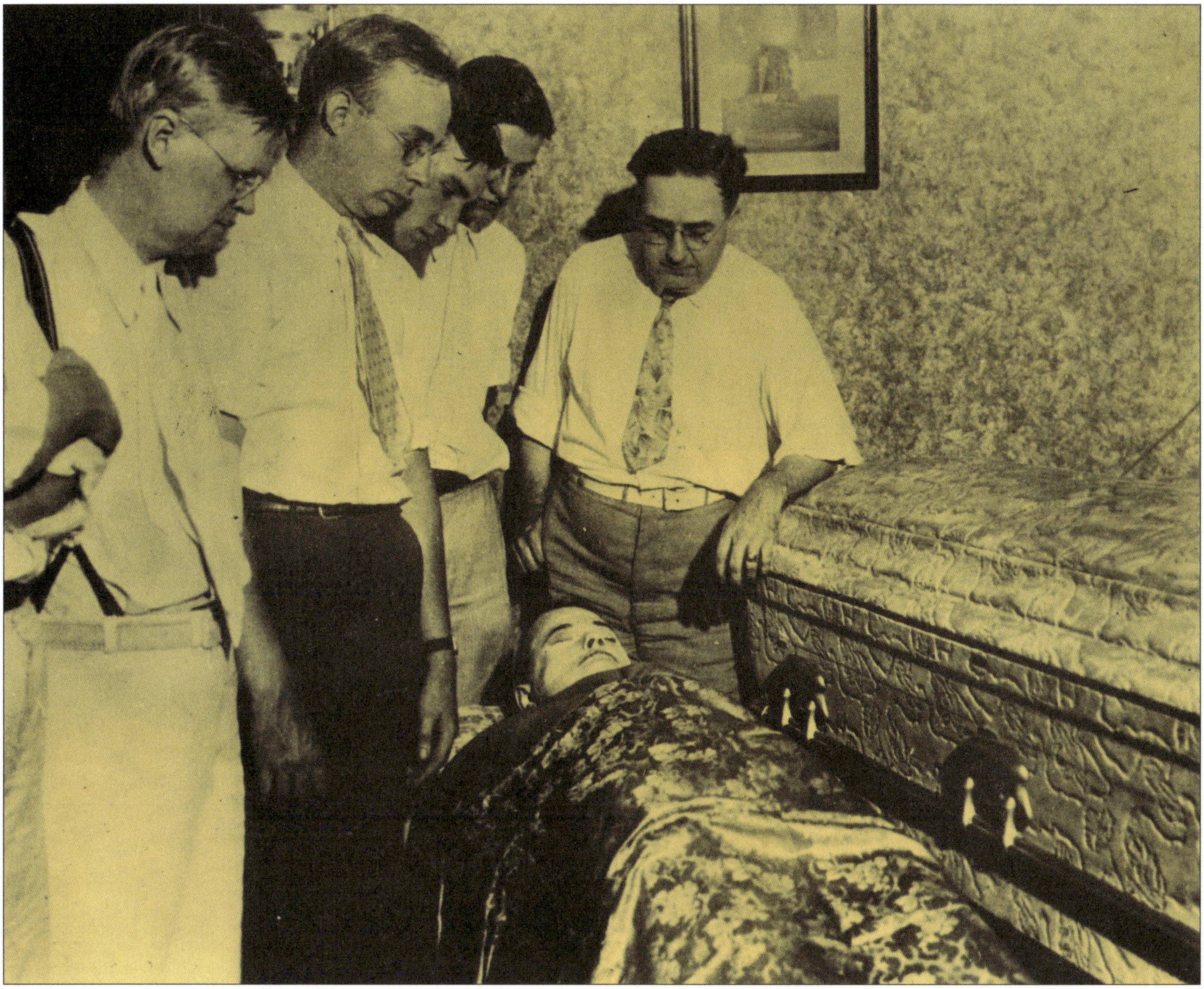

the theatre, women dipped handkerchiefs in his blood, even the hems of their skirts, to remind them that they were there the night the greatest gangster of them all finally got his just desserts.

SOLO MOURNER

"So it is really true?" asked the old man as he opened the door to his farmhouse home. "Are you sure there is no mistake?" Perhaps John Dillinger Snr., father of the slain gangster, was the only true mourner that night. Federal agents knocked on his door to inform him of his son's death just hours later.

"I prayed it would not happen," said the old man at his home in Mooresville, Indiana. "The thing I have prayed for all these months has happened, he's finally dead. If you live life like he lived it I guess that the best he could have hoped for was a quick death. At least this way there won't be folks sitting in judgement on him. Because I am sure he knew what their verdict would be... guilty."

Dillinger's grave in Mooresville became the object of curiosity hunters down the years. His father, fearing that someone would dig up the body, poured concrete laced with scrap iron over it to deter the more ghoulish souvenir hunters, those who would not be happy with a handful of earth or a posy of dried flowers.

It has been hacked about during the passage of time, but no-one has yet penetrated through that barrier. The greatest gangster of them all has lain undisturbed since he was interred – a peace and tranquility in death that he never knew in life.

Above: ***Lying in state in his home town of Mooresville, Indiana. The glory days for the gangsters were over with the death of Dillinger.***

WOMEN DIPPED HANDKERCHIEFS IN HIS BLOOD, EVEN THE HEMS OF THEIR SKIRTS.

DE LA BECKWITH
Third Time Unlucky

Byron De La Beckwith was a man who was born with hate in his heart and racist mumbo-jumbo in his mind. For more than 30 years he had managed to get away with the murder of a rising civil rights leader in the deep south but changing times and new attitudes brought him to justice… and jail.

Byron De La Beckwith was a man born with hate in his heart and bigotry burned deep in his soul. In America's old south he was raised a "Klucker" – the slang term among non-disciples for the Knights of the Ku Klux Klan, the white supremacists who strayed far beyond fancy dress in bedsheets and pointy hats to wreak their own brand of evil.

As organised terrorists who believed only in the supremacy of the white race they were – sometimes still are – responsible for bombings, lynchings and other murders. Not that they ever saw it as murder. Negroes to them – particularly back in the 1960s when the civil rights movement was "interfering" in the way the Dixieland states did things – were the lesser race, a breed for whom there could be no human compassion or decency.

They saw their extermination as the next best thing to where they once had them – under the heel of their boots. And nowhere was the stifling heat of oppression, the cruel vindictiveness of America's own brand of apartheid, more virulent and more apparent than in the city of Jackson, Mississippi, in 1963.

On a sultry June night Byron De La Beckwith murdered a young civil rights worker whose only calling was to bring basic human dignities to blacks denied them long after the last bugles had blown across the battlefields of the civil war. Byron De La Beckwith walked free from court where he was tried for the young man's murder – and walked free a second time months later. But the shot that snuffed out Medgar Evers' life was destined to be heard down three decades. And finally its ricochet got the murderer who is now serving life behind bars after scoffing at justice for 30 long years.

It was hot in Jackson on that June night as bugs danced around the humming street lights and creaking air conditioners across town struggled to keep ahead in the fight against the high temperature and humidity.

THE SHOT THAT SNUFFED OUT MEDGAR EVERS' LIFE WAS DESTINED TO BE HEARD DOWN THREE DECADES

Opposite: ***Byron de la Beckwith, racist murderer.***

Below: ***Beckwith in 1963, six years after the 'good ole boy' network of racist police, judges and jurors had saved his hide.***

Medgar Evers was in his second floor office overooking Lynch Street, clearing up paperwork in his job as the field secretary of the Mississippi branch of the National Association for the Advancement of Coloured People. These may have been Camelot days in Washington with the Kennedy administration working fast and furiously to dismantle the bureacracy of discrimination which existed across the deep south, but Evers was a front line warrior in the battle; it was he who protested at the separate lunch counters in restaurants and stores for blacks and whites, the "no blacks" signs at hotels, the signs which forbade humans of different colour from drinking from the same water fountain.

As an officer in this war he was used to harassment and threats, and often without joking said that the most valuable weapon in his arsenal was his Oldsmobile which he often used to escape from hostile towns where the local good ol' boys didn't take kindly to uppity niggers like him. Before his death he said: "Someone's been following me wherever I go. And I am getting plenty of calls. They say I am going to end up dead soon. One man who called was obviously holding a pistol. He spun the cylinder so I could hear it was a revolver. Then he said: 'This is for you.' I said to him: 'Well, when my time comes I am ready.' And I am. If I die it will be in a

Above and Below: ***Beckwith relied on the racism of his fellow white men to get him off the hook. Here the all-white jury enters the courtroom on the first day of the original trial.***

good cause." It was just eight nights later that his prophesy came true. After he finished up his paperwork he drove to his home in the still night, looking forward to seeing his wife and three small children who were waiting up for him. As he walked to the front door of his home a hunting rifle used usually to shoot deer cracked in the still night and he fell before he had got the key into the lock. At 37, he had become one of the martyrs in the war against racism, dead in the heat of the night on June 12 1963.

"You have got to understand," said Robert Moses, a former leader of the black action group The Student Nonviolent Coordinating Committee, in attempting to explain away why there was no justice for him following his death, "that Mississippi in 1963 was a police state. It was a state where its elected officals promoted racism and all the terror that went along with it. Medgar worked right in the middle of this terror, surrounded by all the violence used by the state to keep people in line."

A BORN FIGHTER

Yet Medgar was born to lead his people in the fight for justice. One of the defining moments of his life came when, as a nine-year-old boy in his hometown of Decatur in the same state, he witnessed the KKK lynching of a black man wrongly accused of raping a white woman. He recalled: "He was a friend of my daddy's and we saw him strung up. The man's clothing remained in the field where it stayed a very long time. For ages his clothes were still there, slowly rotting in the wind and the rain, long after he had been cut down and buried. I used to see them whenever I went hunting and I always remembered.

"I made a pact to myself then that I would grow up and try my best to stop this ever happening again." After a spell in the U.S. Army he returned to Civvy Street. He attended a black agricultural college but was denied entry to the University of Mississippi law school because of his colour. Ironically he was instrumental in dismantling the college's system of apartheid the year before he was killed.

It was in 1954 that he first joined the NAACP and his first job was persuading scared negroes to go to city halls to register to vote – bastions of white supremacy that most feared to go near, let alone enter. He braved mobs who spat on him, bullies with billy clubs at the crossroads into town who smashed his car up and then smashed his face up; he endured the taunts and the threats and the abuse with only his dignity and his sense of right intact. He recalled picking up an elderly black hitch-hiker who kept his eyes down on the floor of the car for the whole journey as he kept repeating over and over in a mantra fashion: "Yessir, the best friend a negro man ever had was a southern white gentleman. Yessir." Medgar said: "I had to tell him it was not a view I shared. And I said I aimed to make it my life's work to prove him wrong."

That dream died on that hot still night because Medgar Evers, visionary, had col-

Above: ***This was the lot of many blacks in the deep south – no trial, no jury, no judges. Just a lynching.***

HE BRAVED MOBS WHO SPAT ON HIM AND BULLIES WITH BILLY CLUBS AT THE CROSSROADS INTO TOWN WHO SMASHED HIS CAR UP

Above: ***The Ku Klux Klan, racists who continued to haunt, persecute and murder blacks in the deep south long after the Civil War was over.***

lided with the philosophy of Byron De La Beckwith, bigot. A self confessed white supremacist, working as a fertilizer salesman, De La Beckwith was a decorated World War Two veteran who served in the bloody battle for the Japanese-held island of Tarawa as a trained sniper. Hunting in the woods around Jackson, he kept his eye in and boasted to friends that he was able to hit a running deer at 1,000 yards. Picking off a member of the race he despised at a distance of 30 feet would have been no problem at all.

DE LA BECKWITH HARBOURED FANTASY NOTIONS OF BEING AN HEIR TO A GREAT CONFEDERATE GENERAL

De La Beckwith harboured fantasy notions of being an heir to a great Confederate general and his home in Greenwood, 90 miles from Jackson, was cluttered with the self-glorifying paraphenalia of the obsessive. He had Dixieland stars-and-bars flags, a field-grey kepi and a musket rifle as used by an infantryman at the watershed battle of Gettysburg. He also stockpiled the literature of hate – pamphlets that he handed out at shopping centres warning against the perils of "race mixing". On one occcasion he wrote to his local newspaper: "When you get to heaven you will find me in the part that has a sign saying 'for whites only'. And, if I go to Hades, I am going to raise all hell over Hades until I get to the white section. I do believe in race segregation like I believe in God. I shall make every effort to rid the United States of America of race integrationists until the day I die. There can be no place for the mongrel negroid races defiling and diluting the blood of American whites."

Such a diatribe in a newspaper in any "normal" town would have instantly brought the author to the attention of the local police department with a strong warning to officers to keep a close watch on the person responsible. But in the twisted atmosphere of Jackson, De La Beckwith was a friend of many policemen, many of

whom shared his not-unique outlook about black people. That is why the investigation into the death of the most prominent civil rights worker in the state of Mississippi was not pursued with anything that could be termed vigour.

PRESIDENTIAL BACKING

Four days after his death, as the JFK administration pledged the full weight of federal law to pursue his killer, Evers was laid to rest in Arlington National Cemetery, the final resting place for American heroes which would later that year receive the body of the president, himself a victim of another sniper with another rifle.

The local police were slow to act but a federal investigation team was soon on the scene and all clues pointed to the man who couldn't bear blacks in his world. The bullet found in the victim matched his rifle, he was seen in Jackson that day, the gun disappeared shortly afterwards and De La Beckwith's car tyre marks were found in town near to where Evers was slain. He was charged with murder but the first trial turned into a celebration of racism.

An indication of how things were going to go came on day one of the trial when the prosecutor, William Waller, asked prospective jurors: "Do you think it is a crime to kill a nigger in the state of Mississippi?" Anyone who seemed to hesitate, or to think it an unreasonable question, was immediately excluded, but there can be no doubt that most of the 12 good men and true who were to sit in judgement on De La Beckwith were just as bigoted as he was. De La Beckwith denied he had killed Evers, but used the dock as a pulpit to preach his gospel of hatred.

He said that he was at home 90 miles away when the killing occurred – and produced three upstanding police officers to testify that they had seen him in Greenwood just like he said. The first trial in 1964 ended in a hung jury and a mistrial was declared. There was a second trial the same year with the same result.

At the end of the second courtroom hearing De La Beckwith had practially become a folk hero to the white racists of Mississippi. He was even greeted outside court by the Governor of the state, Ross Barnett, who shook his hand and wished him well!

Such endorsement of his actions later encouraged De La Beckwith to run for the position of Lieutenant Governor, but the majority of voters had the good sense to reject him and his rantings.

THE JFK ADMINISTRATION PLEDGED THE FULL WEIGHT OF FEDERAL LAW TO PURSUE MEDGAR EVERS' KILLER

Left: ***Medgar Evers, a devoted family man and a rising star of the civil rights movement that sought to bring equality and liberty to all negroes in America.***

Below: ***Evers, with the 'End Brutality' sign around his neck, is arrested in Jackson, Mississippi, shortly before his murder.***

Above: ***John F. Kennedy, president, right, speaks with brother Robert at the White House about bringing down the deep-rooted racism that infected so much of America.***

The verdicts were, of course, of little surprise to Evers' widow Myrlie and his three small children. They had been taught by Medgar to lie on the floor if they heard gunfire at their home – once the target of a firebomb attack and all had lain prostrate with fear in their house the night he died at midnight on the doorstep.

"I wanted justice," said Myrlie, "but I was pragmatic enough to realise that it would probably never come. He grinned in court, gesticulated, used the word nigger like a hammer to bash us with.

"He was disgusting, and lining up on his side were all the forces of the state. I thought that I will die and my children would die without ever seeing justice done for him."

"HE GRINNED IN COURT, USED THE WORD NIGGER LIKE A HAMMER TO BASH US WITH. HE WAS DISGUSTING"

Byron De La Beckwith went back to his salesman job and married twice more in his lifetime. He was always unrepentant to the last about his racist ways, declaring that God would ultimately justify his segregationist views. But he couldn't leave it all to God. In 1979 he was arrested with bomb-making equipment and maps marking the home of a prominent Jewish leader in New Orleans – Jews, in the twisted philosophy of Byron De La Beckwith, having as little right to life as negroes. During his time in jail he couldn't resist talking to anyone who would listen about his twisted feelings on the "lesser races"... and about how he had gotten away with murder back in 1964.

SPECIAL RESEARCH

While he was doing his boasting a man who was nine-years-old at the time of Medgar Evers death was doing his research. Bobby DeLaughter had never even heard of the name of the dead man until he finished law school 13 years later. And then he became engrossed by the case, by the searing injustice of it all which he thought blemished all Mississippians and all southerners as being violent, racist rednecks. When he graduated he swore to himself that he would do everything in his power to re-open the case – and he did. "The big problem," he said, "was evidence 30 years after the fact. The murder weapon had disappeared, for instance, and I was keen to get it back.

"One day I recalled that my father-in-law, a Mississippi judge named Russell Moore III, had once shown me a rifle he kept in a closet. 'This is from one of the old civil rights cases,' said Judge Moore, unaware at what a trophy he really had, and indicating that he had taken the rifle home as a souvenir. By the time I remembered that he had shown it to me he was dead, so I went around to my mother-in-law's, checked the same gun and found that it matched the one on the records for De La Beckwith. Everthing was starting to fall into place. Police ballistic records were intact so it was a valuable piece of evidence to have." By now the boy who was nine when it happened was a man burning for justice on the staff of the district attorney's office. It was in his power to bring a new case and he intended to.

The key to getting trial number three came in 1990 when six new witnesses stepped forward to say that De La Beckwith had boasted to them during the years since the killing of how he was the hitman – of how he waited in bushes outside his home until he showed up and pulled the trigger.

The most compelling testimony came from Mark Reilly, a 36-year-old prison hospital guard in Baton Rouge, Louisiana, who guarded the suspect in 1979. Mr. Reilly, in a sworn affadavit which he later repeated at De La Beckwith's February 1994 trial, said: "He boasted of having killed 'that uppity nigger', and said that he had influence in Mississippi that protected him from ever being found guilty or of being prosecuted again."

As well as this damning testimony came even more concrete proof – De La Beckwith's fingerprints on the telescopic sights of the hunting rifle that had turned up again after so many "lost" years.

De La Beckwith was a man living in a timewarp, an anachronism in the modern age who believed that the juries who judged him in the heat and dust of 1963 would be around to listen to his bilge in 1994. He relied on the testimony of the three police officers – two of them now dead, one who turned up in person – to again place him 90 miles from the murder scene when the killing was carried out. Such evidence was seen as suspect to say the least in the enlightened 1990s, especially given the ballistic evidence. The only thing which marked this trial out as different from the others was De La Beckwith's silence in the dock. Although an unrepentant racist still, he acquiesced to his lawyer's demands to stay silent throughout the week-long trial.

THE FINAL VERDICT

At 10.33am on February 5 1994 the Civil War which had started in 1861 finally ended in Mississippi when jurors filed back into the courthouse from which Byron De La Beckwith had twice mocked justice and declared him guilty of murder. Eight blacks and four whites had judged him this time and there was no return to the "good ol'boy" days of the 1960s. The six witnesses, said the jurors afterwards, who told of his boasting, had sealed it for them. In six and-a-half hours they found the twisted old man guilty "beyond reasonable doubt'.

DE LA BECKWITH BOASTED OF HOW HE WAS THE HITMAN – OF HOW HE WAITED IN BUSHES AND PULLED THE TRIGGER

Two women in the front of the court were most affected by the verdict. One was the widow of Medgar Evers, one the third wife of Byron De La Beckwith. "He didn't do it, he's innocent," said Thelma Beckwith, tears streaming down her face for the man who had cheated justice – and the death penalty – for so long. Now, because of a change in the law, he couldn't be sentenced to die, just a life sentence instead. "Yes! Yes!" screamed the widow who has heard the shot that claimed her husband's life for 30 long years. "It's been a long journey," said Myrlie Evers, looking to the sky. Then she addressed a long-dead hero with the words: "I've gone the last mile, Medgar – but it was worth it. This will send a message to all racists who hide behind sheets and hoods.

"It won't bring you back, honey. But I hope it makes you rest in heaven a little easier."

Below: ***Mrs Evers weeps at the graveside of her slain husband during his funeral.***

RICHARD SPECK
The Nurse Killer

Rarely has a human being sunk so low as Richard Speck, who unleashed a night of horror on a nurses' hostel in Chicago, turning a peaceful dormitory into a human abattoir, killing eight carers sadistically and mercilessly. It was described as "the crime of the century" by horrified experts.

Richard Speck died on Thursday December 5 1991 at the age of 49. He passed away in the prison wing of the Statesville Correctional Centre in Joliet, Illinois, after apparently suffering a heart attack. The death of just another con in America's overcrowded prison system is not usually a signal for prime-time news and massive coverage in the daily papers. But Richard Speck was a man who made history – a man who brought the term "mass murderer" and "thrill killer" into the American lexicon.

On a hot July night in Chicago this aimless drifter, his arms tattooed with the legend "Born to Raise Hell", broke into a nurses' hostel, tied up eight nurses and one by one systematically killed them, raping one in the process. Only one young woman escaped the night of incredible bloodlust, living to see the monster who slaughtered her friends say in court "not guilty".

But there could never be any doubt what the verdict would be – a resounding guilty in less than 55 minutes of deliberation. Speck was sentenced to death for his crime but the state, in a moment of mercy which he never afforded his pleading victims, commuted his sentence to life imprisonment. Jack Wallenda, a 65-year-old retired Chicago detective who had helped catch Speck, was one of those both gladdened and saddened by his passing – glad that he had gone, sad that he had not been executed. "He died an easy death as far as I am concerned," said Wallenda. "I had hoped that sucker would suffer a long time. The pain he caused the families of those dead girls was beyond belief."

James Fox, a professor at Northeastern University in Boston, Massachusetts, said of him: "The word mass-murderer was hardly in our vocabulary until Richard Speck. The idea that one person could indiscriminately slaughter innocent people was virtually unknown until July 14 1966." On that day Speck the nonentity, the loner, the misfit, earned himself a place in history for all time.

Chicago was hot and humid on that night. The searing summer heat pulsated throughout the city, forcing people into air-conditioned bars or cinemas for relief.

HE TIED UP EIGHT NURSES AND, ONE BY ONE, SYSTEMATICALLY KILLED THEM, RAPING ONE IN THE PROCESS

Opposite: ***The wild, wild face of Richard Speck.***

Below: ***Blood spatters the floor in the nurses' hostel. Rumpled bed clothes and abandoned slippers testify to frantic struggles for life.***

Above: ***The innocent facade of the hostel where Speck claimed his victims.***

Others simply stayed at home by their fans or AC units if they were lucky enough to have them. Choosing to stay home too were nine student nurses, most of them sleeping after long spells on duty at the South Chicago Community Hospital. All was quiet at their house, Jeffrey Manor, a two-storey townhouse, with only the whirring of the electric fans breaking the silence. But they had an appointment with lethal destiny that night – a man out to satisfy his murderous impulses.

Speck was born a misfit and died one. Born in Kirkwood, Illinois, on December 6 1941, his early childhood was marked by brutality at the hands of his drunken father and neglectful mother. By the time he was 20 he had notched up some 20 arrests for burglary, disorderly conduct and public drunkenness. Speck's family moved to Dallas when he was six and he was, by the time he was a teenager, "well known" to the police. He married a 15-year-old named Shirley Malone when he was 20 and fathered one child, but his drinking and his violence increased and she left him, taking their daughter with her. Speck always threatened to kill her if he ever found her in Texas – and police would later say that the only victim he raped in the nurses' home bore a remarkable resemblance to the woman who left him.

IN A BLUR OF NARCOTICS AND BOOZE HE TOOK SOLACE IN SQUALID STRIP BARS AND ENCOUNTERS WITH PROSTITUTES

A LOW-LIFE TALE

He added drugs to his alcohol dependency as he drifted from Texas back to Illinois. In a blur of narcotics and booze he took solace in squalid strip bars and cheap encounters with prostitutes that left him feeling bitter and angry towards all women. Later one would recall: "He liked to talk dirty and make sly remarks that all women were whores. I think he probably hated all women." On the rare occasions that he worked he became a crewman aboard the barges plying the Great Lakes between the USA and Canada, using his wages to buy knives – a lasting obsession up until the day he was caught – and liquor.

Although he would end up in jail for life for killing the nurses, police believe his hatred of women led him to kill at least three others, bringing his human harvest to a grand total of 12. The first to die was Mary Pierce, a barmaid and divorcee who rejected Speck's lewd advances at the Monmouth bar where she worked. On April 10 1966 she disappeared and her body – nude and strangled – was discovered three days later. On April 18 a 65-year-old woman was robbed and raped by a man matching Speck's description, but the ore barge he worked on had sailed away before he could be quizzed.

On May 3 he was back on dry land and rushed to hospital for the emergency removal of his appendix and, while there, befriended a young nurse whom he invited to go swimming. She went with him but later told police: "He had so much hatred in him – he was against everybody and felt that everybody was against him. He was very unhappy." Unhappy enough, police now believe, to murder three more young girls on July 2. He had been dismissed that day for being surly to the skipper of an ore boat and went on a bender back on shore. That day three young girls disappeared at Indiana Harbor. They had been wearing swimsuits and their clothes were discovered in the back of their parked cars. They were never seen again and police believe that Speck's monstrous lust claimed them in a bizarre training run before he moved on to the nurses in Chicago.

"HE HAD SO MUCH HATRED IN HIM – HE WAS AGAINST EVERYBODY AND FELT THAT EVERYBODY WAS AGAINST HIM"

Below: ***Police Superintendent Oliver Wilson holds up the wanted picture of Speck at a news conference before he was captured.***

A MIXTURE OF HEROIN AND BOOZE, SCORED FROM A JUNKIE, LED HIM OUTSIDE THE NURSES' HOME SHORTLY AFTER MIDNIGHT

Speck washed up in Chicago on July 10, virtually penniless and in search of work. He went to the National Maritime Union seeking a passage on a vessel bound for New Orleans. He was told to return in two days' time to fill out an application form, but left behind his name and the telephone number of his sister where a message could be left for him, even though he was living in a sleazy hotel not far away. A mixture of heroin and booze, scored from a junkie on nearby Dearborn Street, led him outside the nurses' home at shortly after midnight on July 13. Brandishing a knife and a pistol he waved them in the face of 23-year-old Filipino student nurse Corazon Amurao. "I'm not going to hurt you," he lied. "I am only going to tie you up. I need some money to move to New Orleans."

He moved through the house and put Corazon in a room where three nurses were sleeping. He made them get up then herded the four into another bedroom where two more were asleep. Three more came home from dates within an hour until he had nine captives, all trussed up and lying on the floor. Bound and gagged in front of him, the girls looked with wide-eyed terror as he sat on the edge of a bed menacingly running his finger up and down the blade of his knife. The killing was about to begin.

Twenty-year-old Pamela Wilkening was untied first and led into another room where she was stabbed in the chest and strangled with a strip of sheet. He went back next for 20 year-old Mary Jordan and 21-year-old Suzanne Farris, guiding both women into a different bedroom. There he stabbed Jordan three times – in the heart, neck and eye – before butchering Farris with multiple stab wounds and strangling, then shredding her underclothes with his blade which he left laying around her.

Nina Schmale, 24, was next. Speck ordered her into an adjoining bedroom, slashing her throat and strangling her to death. While he was engaged in his berserk quest for blood the nurses left alive were wriggling under the beds in the room in a bid to avoid detection, but only Corazon, who had answered the door, would survive.

THE ONLY HIDING PLACE

She had wriggled under a bed in a darkened corner and was forced to watch in silence as Valentina Paison, 23, and Marlita Gargullo, 22, were the next to die. Paison died with one deep stab wound to the throat while Gargullo was stabbed four times and finally finished off by strangulation. Patricia Matusek, 22, died next after she was viciously kicked in the stomach and strangled to death. It was Gloria Davy, the last victim, who police said bore an uncanny resemblance to the wife he hated so much. She was the only one subjected to rape for close to half-an-hour before she too was murdered.

At 5.00 am Corazon, in a state of almost paralytic shock, listened for noises and decided that he had finally gone. She rolled out from under the bed and walked into one of the adjoining rooms... to see the girls that only hours before she had been joking and laughing with butchered like farmyard animals. She ran to the balcony in hysterics

Below: ***The skid-row hotel where Speck was found.***

and yelled: "All my friends are dead! He killed them all!" A couple who were walking their dog just below thought that she was a potential suicide jumper and beseeched her not to take her life. One of them telephoned for the police who broke in the door of the boarding house... and discovered the horrific massacre within. "The man had behaved exactly like a fox in a poultry house," said a police officer at the scene. "It was killing for the joy of killing."

It was some five hours after she had been treated for deep shock that Corazon Amurao was able to tell police about the killer – that he stank of alcohol, that his face was pock-marked and that he bore tattoos that told he was 'Born to Raise Hell'. The knots that were tied on the victims told police two other interesting things – that the killer was possibly a seaman and an ex-convict, because he had expertly tied the hands to face away from each other behind the girls' backs, much in the way that a pair of handcuffs works. Corazon was also able to recall that the murderer had spoken of getting money to go to New Orleans.

Routine police enquiries were all

Above: ***Corazon Amurao, the Filipino nurse who lived through the night of murder, hearing her friends die one by one at the hands of Speck.***

Left: ***Mrs Margaret Lindbergh, Speck's mother, arrives for the start of his trial.***

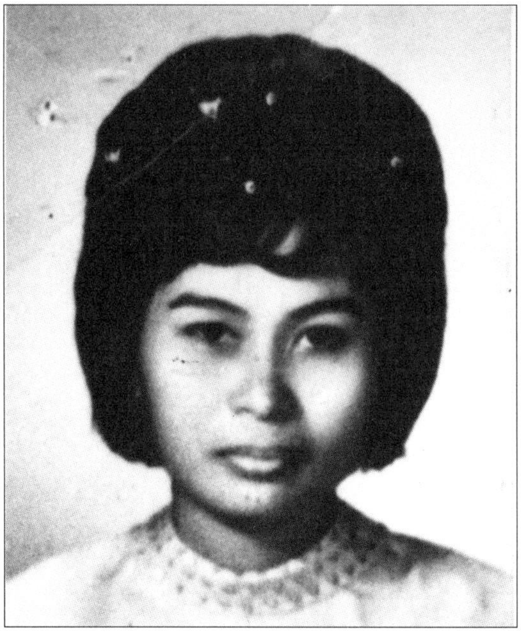

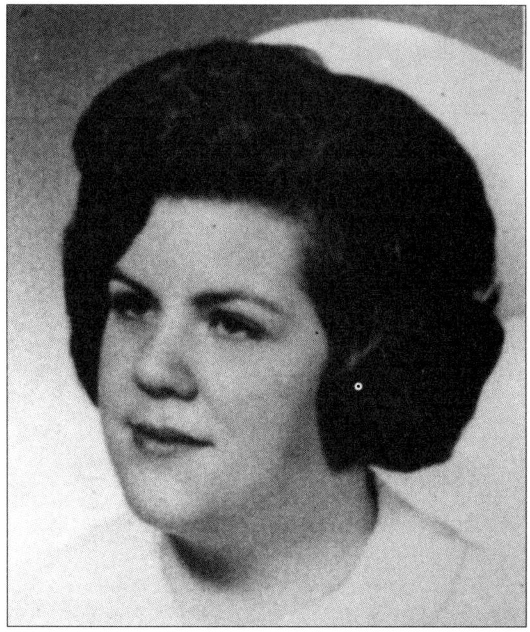

Left and Right: ***Valicentia Passon and Pamela Wilkening, two of the first victims.***

SOME KIND OF FERAL SIXTH-SENSE MADE SPECK BREAK THE APPOINTMENT HE HAD TO SHOW UP FOR THE JOB

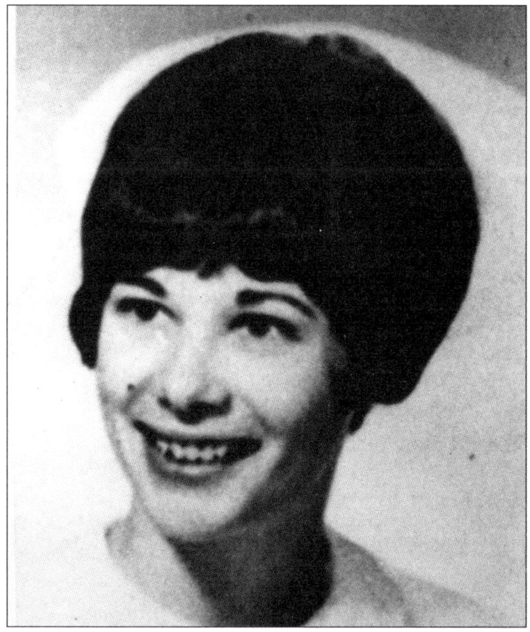

Left and Right: ***Susan Parris and Patricia Matusek, two more of the nurses who were beaten, raped, strangled and stabbed by the maniac Speck.***

HE PRESSED A HUNTING KNIFE AGAINST THE THROAT OF THE BARMAN, SAYING: "THIS HAS KILLED MORE THAN YOU KNOW"

that were needed to get on Speck's trail. The seaman's mission where he had gone for work was nearby and there the police found staff who confirmed the presence there of a tattooed, pock-marked man who had been seeking passage on a ship to New Orleans – together with a name and a telephone number for him.

One of the clerks there also explained how the drunken Speck had boasted of "going to spy on nurses" who he had heard sunbathed with little on in the grounds of the house. The police rang the number of Speck's sister declaring that a job was now available for him and he called back three hours later – during which time Corazon had identified him from his photo attached to the application form. But some kind of feral sixth-sense made Speck break the appointment he had to show up for the job.

Police in return began trawling the seedier hotels where sailors and derelicts traditionally stayed. One hotel was found in North Dearborn Street but he checked out half-an-hour before they arrived. On 15 July he had been in a bar where he pressed a long-bladed hunting knife against the throat of the barman, professing to all around in the rough pub: "This has killed more than you know!" A policeman was called the same night to another cheap hotel after a prostitute had complained of a

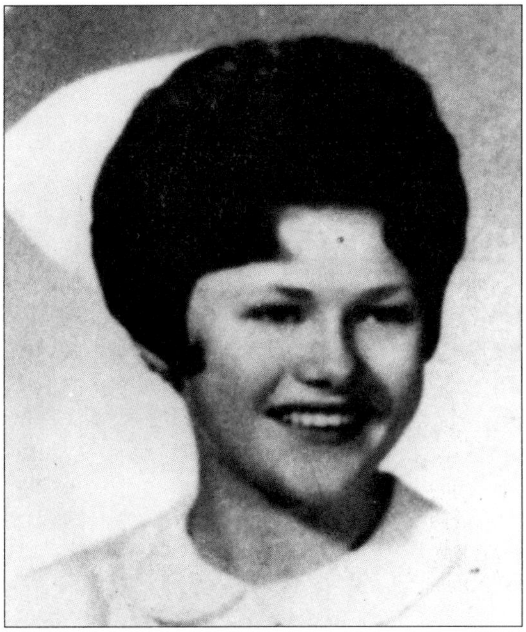

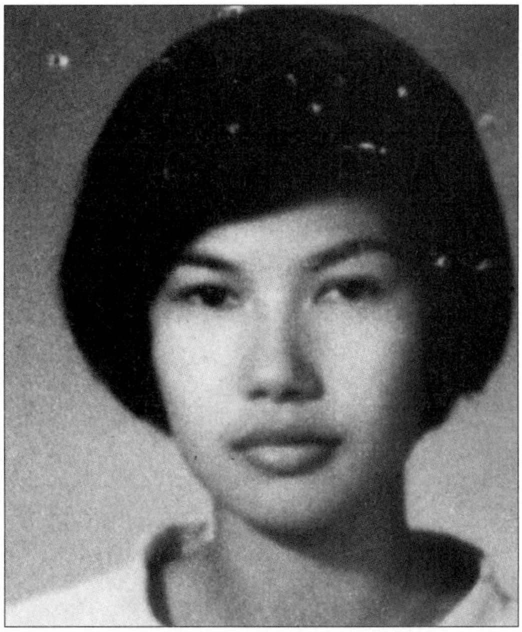

Left and Right: *Marlita Gargullo and Mary Jordan. Surviving nurse Corazon Amurao heard their death cries from her hiding place beneath a bed.*

HE SLASHED HIS WRISTS AND KNOCKED ON A NEIGHBOURING DOOR FOR DRINK, COLLAPSING AT THE FEET OF A STUNNED GUEST

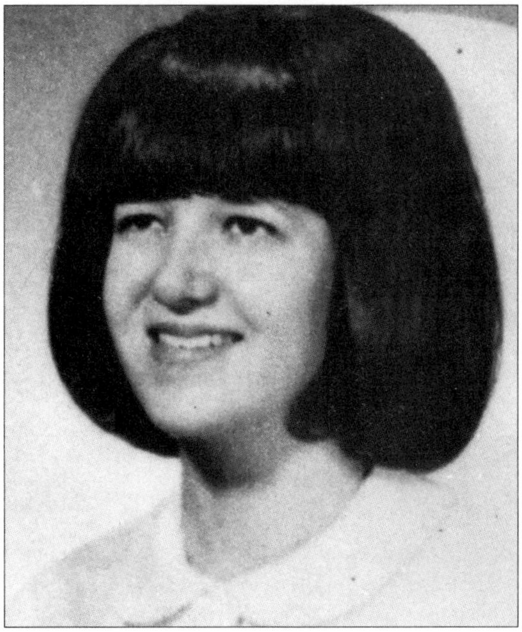

Left and Right: *Nina Schmale and Gloria Davy, the other two victims, making a total human-harvest of eight in all for the crazed killer.*

lunatic with a gun and a knife threatening her life. But crossed wires led the unsuspecting beat officer to confiscate the weapons, let the drunk off with a warning and Speck was allowed to go free!

He was caught after a televised appeal the next day. Speck had gone to the Starr Hotel in West Madison Street where he was spending money stolen from his victims. But he needed the money for the room and was penniless for the drink that he so desperately wanted to stop himself shaking. At midnight, whether suffering from some remorse or alcohol withdrawal symptoms, he slashed his wrists and knocked on a neighbouring door for drink, collapsing at the feet of a stunned guest. Twenty minutes later he was in the emergency room at a hospital where a surgeon recognised the "Born to Raise Hell" motif that had been part of the police TV broadcast. Police were called, he was under arrest and his trial came in April 1967.

Speck's behaviour at his trial was extraordinary. He showed great charm to the pressmen, laughing and joking, earning himself such plaudits as "remarkable" and "witty" from the city's scribes. He pleaded not guilty, hoping to scare the sole surviving witness to the slaughter with a fixed stare and a nonchalant air. There was little forensic evidence to fix him to the scene of

HE PLEADED NOT GUILTY, HOPING TO SCARE THE SOLE SURVIVING WITNESS WITH A FIXED STARE AND A NONCHALANT AIR

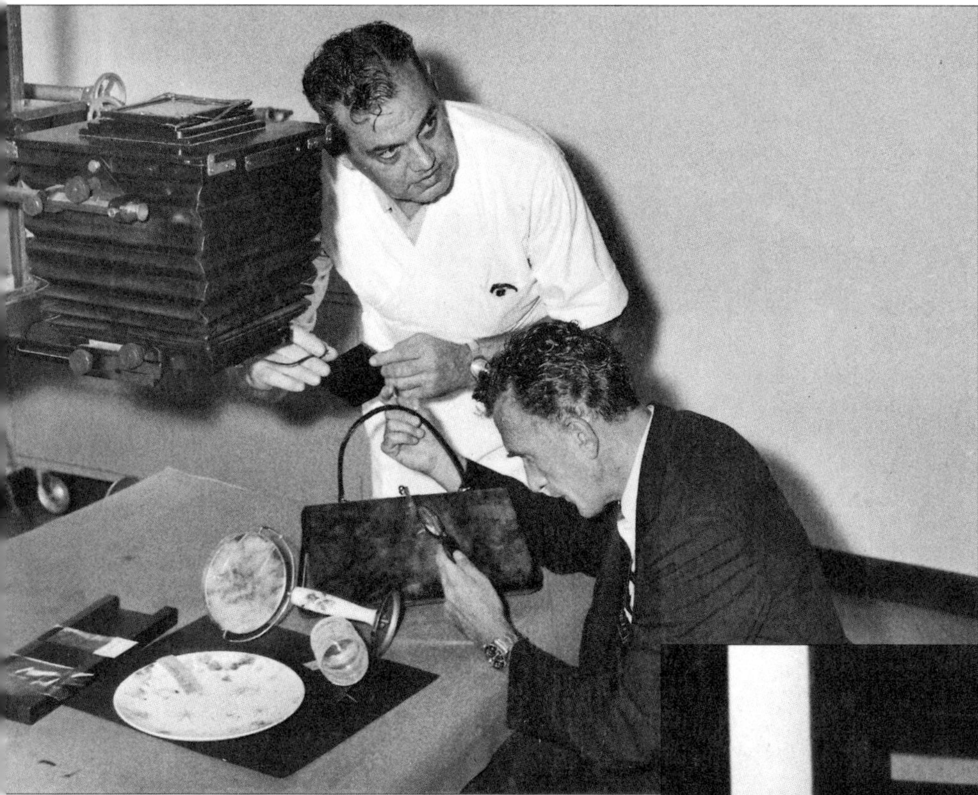

"Eight people and that effeminate homosexual." Speck said he and the second man chose the house in which the nurses lived by accident. And he said that after the killings he later killed his "accomplice" by shooting him in the face six times before dumping his body. Joseph De Leonardi, the Chief of Detectives who had led the hunt to capture him, said: "It is the rantings of a madman. There was no accomplice. Speck forgot that one of his victims survived. She testified at his trial there was only one man – and there was. There can be only one release from eternal suffering for the families of his victims – that is when he dies."

In 1987 Speck actually applied for parole – a bid that sent shock waves through America. Having pleaded not

the crime – and claimed he had been on a drinking bender when the attacks took place. But there was too much circumstantial evidence. He was sentenced to a total of 600 years in jail by a jury who came back in record time for someone accused of so many crimes. He looked at the jury and said: "No problem."

A STRANGE CONFESSION

It wasn't until 1978 that Speck had a change of heart and admitted to the Chicago slaughter – but in a weird twist only to seven of the eight murders. He said that they would still be alive had one of them not spat into his face and that the last killing was carried out "by an effeminate homosexual accomplice". In a rambling interview given to the Chicago Sunlife he said: "Yeah. I killed them. I stabbed and choked them. If that one girl didn't spit in my face they would all be alive today. She spit in my face and said she'd pick me out of a line-up... I just blew it. I can't even tell you what she looked like. She got stabbed in the heart."

Speck said that before the killings he and his accomplice drank whisky and he shot heroin into his arm. "I never shot heroin before so eight people got killed," he said.

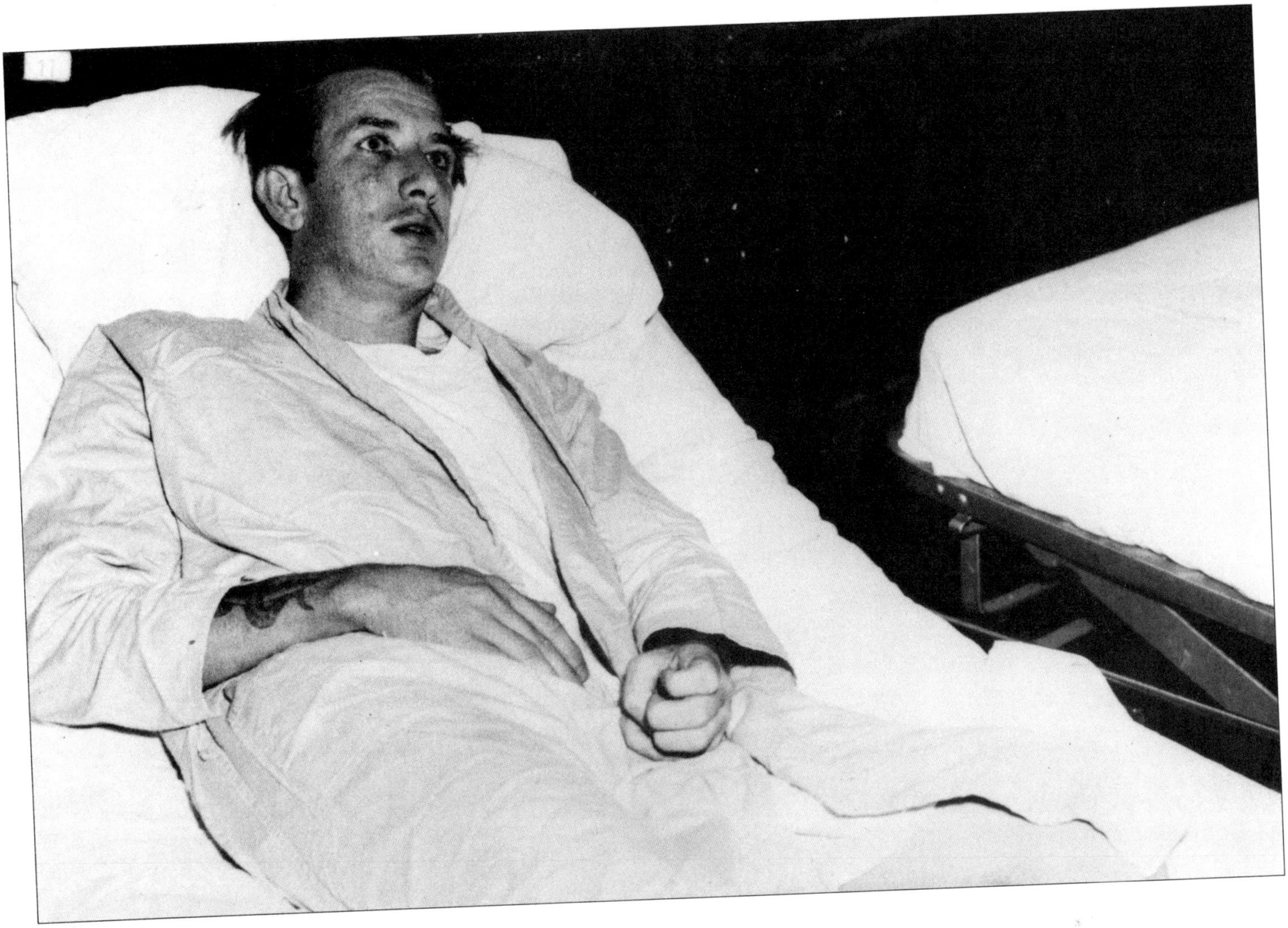

guilty to the murders, then having changed his story to admit them, the act of seeking freedom was almost more than the families of the dead girls could take.

"The parole of Richard Speck would devalue life since he took the lives of eight individuals who became nurses because they valued and loved the lives of others," said Ellen Stannish, a classmate of the girls. "We have lived with fear, shock, loss and sorrow since that day he has struck. The only consolation to us is that he is behind bars. Granting him parole would be too much to take."

Not only classmates and family but ordinary Americans were sparked into action. People who had never written a letter of complaint before found themselves angrily addressing the Governor of Illinois in a bid to block his release. Lena Wilkening, the mother of one slain student, said: "A mass murderer like that is always a mass murderer. He must stay there until the day he dies. You can't punish him enough because he snuffed out eight lives and murdered five of their parents too – the strain of knowing what he had done to their loved ones killed them as surely as if he had strangled and stabbed them too."

Above: ***Speck, the tell-tale tattoo showing on his arm, in a prison medical ward before his trial.***

Opposite Top: ***Forensic experts go to work on the personal belongings of the murdered nurses to pin the crimes on Speck.***

Opposite Below: ***The madman has his day in court, but it doesn't save him from a guilty verdict.***

"THEY WENT LIKE LAMBS TO THE SLAUGHTER. YOU CAN SEE WHY THIS WAS CALLED THE CRIME OF THE CENTURY"

Gayle Shines, an assistant district attorney for the city, was instrumental in getting parole refused. "They went like lambs to the slaughter," he said. "You can see why this was called the crime of the century and why he was convicted, beyond reasonable doubt by a jury of his peers, of it. A parole is a matter of clemency and grace, not a right. We say that Speck should die in prison and be buried in a prison grave.

Eventually, he did, but the legacy of the mass killer lives on in the American psyche. "I think what Speck did succeeded in turning us into a paranoid society," said Chicago criminal psychiatrist Marvin Ziporyn, who examined him at length before the trial. "Thank goodness the jury had the good sense to convict him first time around, otherwise he could have gone on drifting and killing. Then his acts of wickedness could have been tenfold."

A TIME TRIAL
The Baronet's Tragedy

Aristocrat Sir Trevor Dawson ended his life when his financial empire collapsed and he became depressed at the prospect of being unable to care for his family. A jury had to decide the crucial question of whether he died before or after midnight – a verdict on which depended a small fortune.

Merchant banker Sir Trevor Dawson was the kind of man who embraced life with gusto. Rich, handsome, talented, he had amassed a fortune and liked nothing better than to spend it. Among the set who inhabited Whites Club in London, the Cavalry and Guards, Bucks, the MCC, the racecourses of Ascot and Epsom and certain discreet gaming establishments, he was known fondly as "The Galloping Major".

Betting was a serious business to Sir Trevor; he thought nothing of placing £1,000 bets on rank outsiders with long odds, or of cheering himself up when the nags invariably lost with bottles of vintage Dom Perignon champagne at £50 a time.

"Life," he once said, "is for living to the max, and I intend to do so." His lavish tastes were reflected in a number of expensive possessions – there was a leather-upholstered, air-conditioned American Cadillac with the number plate TD1. There

RICH, HANDSOME, TALENTED, HE HAD AMASSED A FORTUNE AND LIKED NOTHING BETTER THAN TO SPEND IT

Opposite: ***Sir Trevor Dawson was born into a life of privilege.***

Below: ***The London home where Sir Trevor was to end his life.***

Above: ***Sir Trevor in happier times when he was a financial wizard in the city.***

THERE WERE SUITS BY SAVILE ROW TAILORS AND A SOCIAL LIFE THAT READ LIKE A WHO'S WHO OF THE SMART AND FASHIONABLE

was the £350,000 Belgravia flat, in Eaton Square to be precise, one of the prime addresses in England. There was a cottage in the countryside, suits in the closet by the finest Savile Row tailors and a social life that read like a who's who of the smart and fashionable throughout the land. There were, outwardly, no blots on the horizon of this wealthy and privileged man.

But Sir Trevor's financial affairs were something of an iceberg by March 1993. His friends and family saw only the tip of them and presumed that all was well. Beneath the calm surface, however, was fomenting a financial maelstrom that he had no control over. For years he had risen through the ranks of the City of London with ease and grace... before a scandal in 1981 sent a stunning reversal of fortune through his glittering lifestyle. He was by then the investment chief of bankers Arbuthnot Latham and found himself at the centre of unwelcome attention from members of Scotland Yard's Fraud Squad. It was alleged that he took personal advantage of his position in the bank to funnel share profits through the Manchester-based stockbroking firm of Halliday Simpson to private clients' accounts.

Halliday Simpson ceased trading and the scandal caused Sir Trevor's company an estimated £350,000 at least, although there were rumours in certain quarters of the square mile of the city that it was double that amount. In the "old boy" network of London banking there was nothing that Sir Trevor could do but resign.

The resignation changed something within him. Over time he lost his easygoing ebullience and charm and seemed more and more to carry the weight of the world upon his shoulders. He began to frequently tell friends that there "is nothing left to live for". He had many friends and continued to frequent the clubs and haunts. But he sensed that people merely tolerated him, rather than embracing his company. He was, after all, tinged with scandal and in the rarified world in which he moved there were many who considered him the bearer of the mark of Cain.

A MYSTERIOUS AFFAIR

A diabetic and overweight, he continued to drink, but frequently became disoriented. In 1982 he was found lying seriously injured beneath a footbridge at Heathrow Airport. No-one ever got to the bottom of what happened but police believed he jumped from the overpass in a failed bid to kill himself. But he recuperated and returned home to a family whose love for him had not diminished... and to a bank balance that clearly had.

The years of high living had taken a toll on the finances of the galloping major and he began to worry about the future for his 26-year-old spastic son and his wife Caroline. He had parted from Lady Dawson after the financial scandal which forced him from the city, but they remained close friends and were constantly in touch with one another. The old soldier had made enormous amounts of money during his lifetime, but a lifestyle which kept up Cadillacs, Belgravia apartments and country cottages – together with gambling, drinking and dining – needed regular injections of cash, and that was running out. He had not been wise in his investments and the net result was impending financial doom. It led him to attempt suicide once more with an insulin overdose, but all he succeeded in doing was collapsing his lung, putting him on the critical list once more before he made a full recovery.

LIFE MIRRORS ART

In the play *Death of a Salesman* by Arthur Miller, the central, tragic character Willy Loman sees death as the only way out to provide for his family. Loman's logic is that, whereas most families need their husbands and fathers, his needed the money that the insurance on his death could provide. No-one knows whether or not Sir Trevor Dawson had ever read Death of a Salesman, but certainly the path he eventually chose mirrored that of the fictional Loman. The disgraced ex-banker had over £100,000 in life insurance policies, policies that he knew would relieve the great financial stress that was beginning to bear down on his family.

On February 14, Valentine's Day, his chauffeur Harold Munton, who had been with him for many years, dropped him off at the Belgravia flat at 6.00pm at night with instructions to come for him the next day. Once inside the flat he uncorked a bottle of champagne and sat in his favourite armchair where he composed a letter to his wife which read: "There was no other choice if you and Michael were to have any independence and security. I love you and will be with you always." Then Sir Trevor Dawson, a man who served his country in peace and war, took his own life by placing

Above: ***White's Club, London, one of the bastions of the elite to which Sir Trevor Dawson belonged.***

Below Left: ***Sir Trevor was a man for whom the best things in life meant everything – like champagne-soaked days at Ascot.***

HE HAD NOT BEEN WISE IN HIS INVESTMENTS AND THE NET RESULT WAS IMPENDING FINANCIAL DOOM

Above: ***Sir Trevor and his wife Lady Caroline on their wedding day.***

a plastic bag over his head. His weak lungs soon gave out and he suffocated to death.

After such a death in Britain there must be an autopsy and a full inquest presided over by a Crown Coroner. For the death of Sir Trevor Dawson, the inquest would take on immense importance for his widow – because her husband had killed himself either before midnight on the 14th or in the early hours of the 15th. If he had died before midnight, insurance policies that expired that night would be valid and redeemable. If he had died after midnight then his Lomanesque gesture would have been totally in vain. It was left to the nine good men and women of the Coroner's Court to decide such a weighty burden when they assembled to hear the last details of Sir Trevor Dawson's end at the inquest held at Westminster on March 23 1983.

"IN COMMON PARLANCE, SIR TREVOR NEEDED TO DO IT – TO TAKE HIS OWN LIFE – BEFORE MIDNIGHT"

Dr. Paul Knapman, the Westminster Coroner, spoke gravely to the five men and four women who would decide whether or not the tragic baronet had met the deadline. He told them: "Ladies and gentlemen of the jury, this case assumed rather more than incidental importance in determining death. A number of insurance matters involving considerable sums of money may hinge on the date that you decide he died.

"But you must not be swayed by any sympathy for any particular point of view. Just stick to the facts. Sir Trevor knew perfectly well that his life insurance policies expired before the dawn of February 15. In common parlance, he needed to do it – to take his own life – before midnight."

A DATE WITH DEATH

The policies that would have become worthless on that morning totalled £137,500. Three were with Phoenix Assurance, valued at £20,000, £20,000 and £65,000, and one with National Provident for £32,500. All were fully paid and fully redeemable if the insured party died before their expiry on February 15.

First to testify was Sir Trevor's chauffeur Harold Munton who described his former boss as an old-school gentleman. "I dropped him off at 6.00pm and I couldn't detect anything was wrong. The next morning I went into the flat at 11.30am and I found him dead in an armchair. There was a message waiting for me that said: 'Call ambulance on 999.'" The court heard from police how a half-empty champagne bottle was found in the drinks cabinet together with an empty glass at Sir Trevor's side.

Pathologist Professor Keith Simpson, Britain's most eminent expert in his field for some three-plus decades, testified next that the cause of death was asphyxia and that no foul-play was detected. In suspicious cases he said he always takes the temperature of the body.

The body cools at a certain rate after death and the temperature indicates at what time the person died. In this case no temperature was taken, although police surgeon Dr. Roger Durston said that he could have been dead "for many hours". It was a nugget of information not lost on the jury who saw the tearful Lady Dawson in court as she sat intently listening to evidence.

The jury heard that three days before he ended his life, Sir Trevor had called his secretary, Miss Pamela Gleason, and asked her for the expiry dates on one of the policies. Mr. Graham Read, his insurance broker, confirmed the policies, their amounts and the day they expired. Mr. Read said Sir Trevor had written to him about extending his policies. "He said he had had pneumonia and was considering extensions because he was not sure of his health."

Lady Dawson, dressed in black, spoke softly and eloquently before the jury when she was called into the witness box. She said: "My husband and I parted after his business difficulties but we kept in touch by letter and telephone two or three times a week. The last time we met he was very worried about Michael's welfare. Michael is severely retarded and needs constant care. He used to be looked after by my in-laws but they have since died. My home in Wiltshire is owned by the bank and I have to be out of there by March 31."

Ultimately the jury had just the pointer from the police surgeon and Lady Dawson's tragic circumstances to guide them. The Coroner had made it plain that they should not be swayed by personal feelings, although it would be ludicrous to imply that feelings of humanity towards a widow and her disabled son did not exist. After less than an hour of deliberations the jury filed into court to say that Sir Trevor Dawson had taken his own life BEFORE midnight. He had met the deadline – and now Lady Dawson was able to pursue the insurance companies for payment.

LADY DAWSON, DRESSED IN BLACK, SPOKE SOFTLY AND ELOQUENTLY BEFORE THE JURY WHEN CALLED INTO THE WITNESS BOX

Below: ***Lady Caroline, Sir Trevor's widow, after the timetable verdict was brought in.***

MORE HARD WORK

Later her solicitor, Mr. David Long, told pressmen outside the court: "We are grateful to the jury for its decision but this is not the end of the road by any means. We don't foresee any further court action but the next step is to ask the insurance companies for payment." China Cottage, her home near Marlborough that was owned by Barclays Bank, could be saved now. The solicitors said that they would ask the bank to delay its action in re-possessing the property while they pursued negotiations with the insurance companies.

Ultimately, it is unclear whether she received her money; the law on insurance was vague. Bernard Chandler, Secretary of the Life Offices Association, an industry professional body, said: "There are no set guidelines about whether an insurance company will meet a claim in a case of suicide. It depends on the company and the client and the contract which is drawn up between them. Some have suicide clauses, others have a clause saying that no money will be paid if someone commits suicide within a year of the policy's start."

The court's decision was a milestone victory. Crime author Larry Hackett commented: "It was a victory for humanity and common decency. If you look at the plain facts, those jurors did not know any more than the man in the moon about what time Sir Trevor Dawson finally expired. It could have been one minute to midnight or ten minutes to five on the morning that the insurance polices ran out.

"But thanks to grace and intelligence they let a widow facing financial hardship seek out what was owed to her on those policies. British justice has been frequently criticised in recent years, but I don't think anyone can fault the integrity or commonsense of British jurors."

ANNE FRANK
Bringing Nazis to Book

Anne Frank was a Jewish schoolgirl whose eloquent jottings in her diary spoke to a generation that lived beyond the Holocaust that consumed her and her family. Nazi revisionists tried to degrade her memory by branding her diary a fake. It was left to a Nazi hunter to prove them wrong once and for all.

Anne Frank was just an ordinary little schoolgirl, her head filled with dreams and optimism when the Nazis marched into her country in 1940. Because she was Jewish she was forced into hiding with her family, occupying a secret loft in Amsterdam for over two years to escape the trains that took her people east to places like Auschwitz, Dachau and Majdanek. Places for which there was only a one-way ticket. In those years in hiding Anne Frank changed from a naive schoolgirl into a compassionate, sensitive thinker who confided her innermost feelings in a diary. That diary was discovered at the same time she and her family were – on the dreaded day of August 4 1944 when the S.S. came for them. Anne was to die in the Bergen-Belsen concentration camp before the war's end, another painful statistic in the Nazi catalogue of death.

A year after her death in March 1945 her father, who had survived the concentration

SHE WAS FORCED INTO HIDING WITH HER FAMILY, OCCUPYING A SECRET LOFT IN AMSTERDAM FOR OVER TWO YEARS

Opposite: ***Anne Frank, whose diary became a document of massive historical importance.***

Below: ***A close-up of some of the pages of Anne's diary which is now taught in schools around the world.***

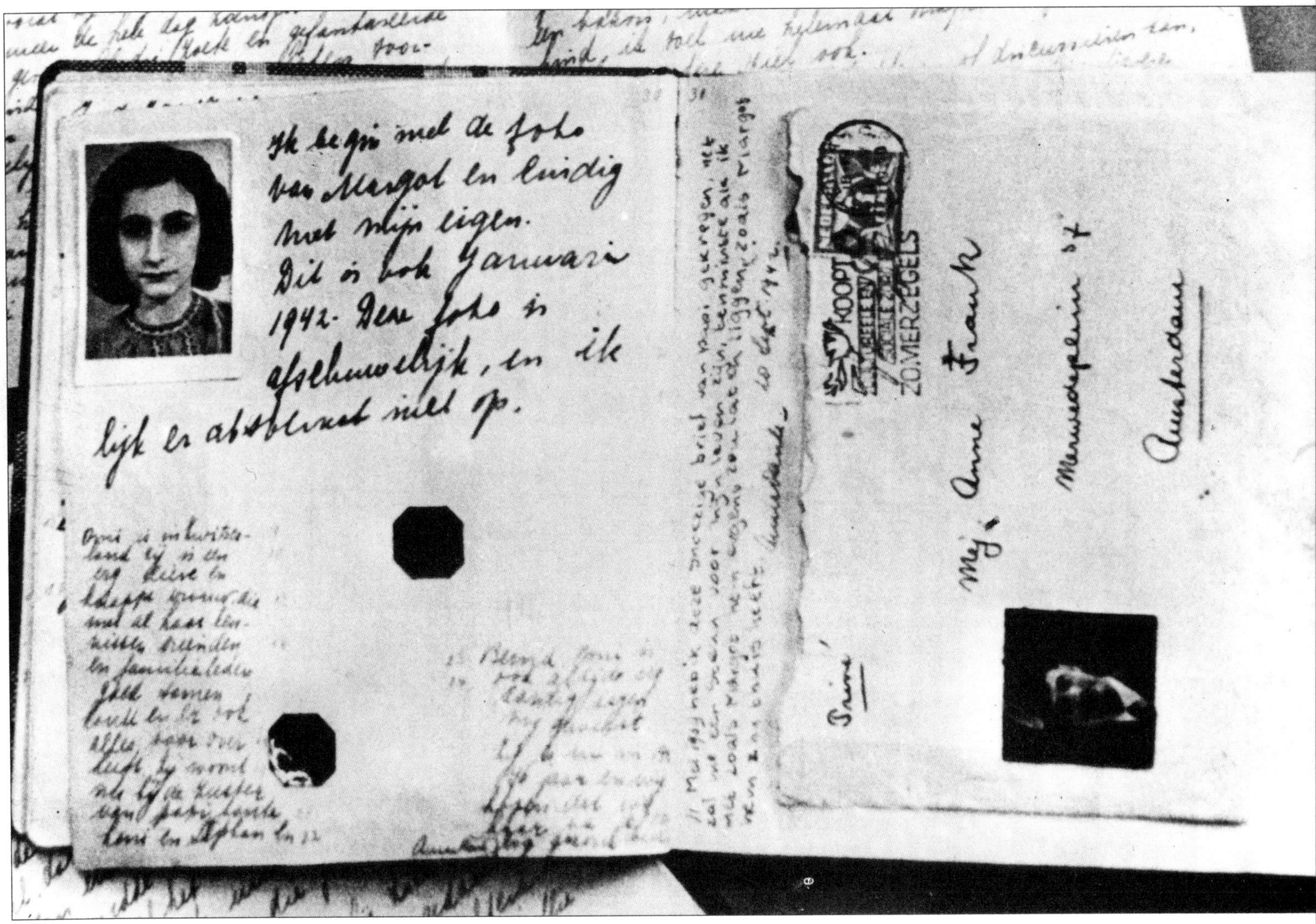

camps, returned to the loft that had given him and his family sanctuary for so long. The diary that the S.S. man had held in his hands as they were marched away lay on the floor, alongside the other pathetic relics of what had once been a happy family life. Soon it was published as *The Diary of Anne Frank*, a book that touched the heartstrings of mankind and shone as a beacon of hope for the human soul. The diary was published in 32 languages, became a stage play and a Hollywood picture and is now taught as literature to scoolchildren around the world who can only wonder at her immense bravery and compassion as she struggled to live normally under the most abnormal circumstances.

Anne Frank was proof positive of the horror that the Nazis inflicted on subjugated peoples. But after the war certain antisemitic elements in Austrian society began to question the veracity of her journal. Just like the "big lie" revisionists who like to pretend that the Holocaust itself was a figment of the allies' imagination – that there was no extermination programme – so the neo-Nazis in postwar society tried to pretend that Anne Frank had never existed.

The smear on her name began in 1958 in Linz, Austria, where anti-semitic demonstrators interrupted a stage performance of *The Diary of Anne Frank.* Leaflets hurled in the aisles of the city's Landstheater read: "The play is a fraud. Anne Frank never existed. The Jews have invented the whole story because they want to extort more restitution money. Don't believe a word of it! It's a fake!" To people like Nazi hunter Simon Wiesenthal, the camp survivor who lost 89 relatives in the Holocaust who devoted himself to tracking down surviving war criminals, the demonstration was a ghastly affront to his sensibility and an appalling victory for facism if it was left to go unanswered.

NAZI APOLOGISTS

Simon Wiesenthal spoke to a meeting of Viennese youth days later and what he heard shocked him. The diary? A clever fake, they insisted. The mass grave she is interred in? Where is the proof, they countered. "Proof," said Wiesenthal. "One would have to produce proof – irrefutable

Above: ***The house where Anne and her family hid from the Nazis for two years is now a shrine to visitors from all over the globe.***

Right: ***Adolf Hitler and his Nazi cronies at a party rally in Nuremberg. His bizarre racial policies sent innocent girls like Anne to his extermination camps.***

THE BOOK TOUCHED THE HEARTSTRINGS OF MANKIND AND SHONE LIKE A BEACON OF HOPE FOR THE HUMAN SOUL

proof that would convince these young sceptics. One would have to tear one single brick out of the edifice of lies that had been constructed then the whole structure would collapse. But to find that one brick... Something occurred to me as I spoke to a young man who doubted its authenticity. Suppose the Gestapo officer who arrested Anne Frank were to be found. Would that be accepted as proof? 'Yes,' he said reluctantly. 'If the man himself admitted it.'" Simon Wiesenthal set out to find that man, to prove beyond all doubt to those who glorified the sick world of Adolf Hitler, that Anne Frank lived.

Above: ***Hitler appeared to be capable of kindnesses to individual children.***

Below: ***Children at Vittel concentration camp, France, after liberation by the US Army.***

A DIFFICULT SEARCH

It was to prove an enormous detective hunt. Since Anne's father had returned to the attic to find the diary many years had elapsed, people had died, records were sketchy. Paul Kraler, a former employee of Anne Frank's father, who took over the company when Jews were forbidden to run businesses, recalled to Wiesenthal that the Amsterdam Gestapo had told him a man named Silvernagl had arrested the family. Yet no such name existed in Austria, so Wiesenthal assumed the v might be a b.

At first he searched in all the known S.S. records for a man named Silbernagel, adding an e to the name too, concentrating on the kind of low-ranking individual who might be ordered to do something as routine as an arrest of hiding Jews. He hired private detectives who ran background

Above: ***The reality of Hitler's superman policies – the living among the dead at Belsen concentration camp.***

checks on the Silbernagels listed. Many showed up but they were either dead, had never been in Holland in service during the war or had rankings too superior to the kind of task alloted to the man who arrested Anne Frank.

For five years the enquiry trundled on, with Wiesenthal struggling for new information while constantly trying to keep tabs on the bigger fish like Eichmann and Mengele who had escaped justice at war's end. He was on the verge of giving up in 1963 when he visited the Anne Frank house in Amsterdam for the first time. He touched the walls that she had touched, drank in the atmosphere of the place where a frightened family had sheltered from the most appalling regime that had ever gained power in a civilised country. He knew then that his search must go on.

On a second visit to Amsterdam the same year he consulted with two officials of the Dutch Insititute for War Documentation. Wiesenthal shared information about missing war criminals and the documents which he worked from, sources, spies, etc., but there was no fresh evidence about the possible wherabouts of a possible S.S. man possibly named Silbernagel.

As he was getting ready to leave the meeting one of the men handed him a 1943 photostated copy of the official S.S. telephone directory for Holland. With the words "here is something to read on the plane that should keep you awake" he had unwittingly handed him the solution to the Anne Frank puzzle. Wiesenthal later

FOR FIVE YEARS THE ENQUIRY TRUNDLED ON, WITH WIESENTHAL STRUGGLING FOR NEW INFORMATION

HE WAS ON THE VERGE OF GIVING UP WHEN HE VISITED THE ANNE FRANK HOUSE IN AMSTERDAM FOR THE FIRST TIME

Right: ***Hitler, at the beginning of his conquest, addresses a Viennese crowd on the glories to come.***

revealed in his memoirs *The Murderers Among Us*: "The flight to Vienna lasted about two hours. I settled back in my seat and looked through the Gestapo directory. I was almost asleep when I turned to the page headed 'IV Sonderkommando'. Under 'IV B4 Joden' I read: 'Kempin, Buschmann, Scherf, Silberbauer.' I was now wide awake! Section IV B4 had handled the round-up and transportation of Jews to death camps. If anyone had tipped off the Gestapo about Jews hiding in Holland the report would inevitably reach this section. All of a sudden the plane seemed to be very slow. I could hardly wait to get to Vienna. I knew that most officials of this section had been recruited from police forces in Germany and Austria."

A STRONG CLUE

Wiesenthal was certain that he was on the trail of the man who arrested Anne and her family and put the mis-spelling of the officer's name down to a mistake. Deciding to chance his hand with a massive bluff, he rang Dr. Josef Wiesinger, head of the department within the Austrian Justice Ministry which handled war crime cases. "I told him," said Wiesenthal, "rather boastfully I'm afraid, that I had found the Gestapo man who had arrested Anne Frank. 'He's a Viennese policeman called Silberbauer,' I said."

Wiesinger did not call the bluff of the world's most famous Nazi hunter; instead he agreed to go through records and asked Wiesenthal to get back to him at a later date, although he did not hold out much hope of finding someone "who was posted somewhere else in Europe 19 years ago."

Wiesenthal, whose own offices were in Vienna – he preferred to work there because of the massive support the Viennese had given to Hitler during his rise and subsequent years at the top – did not know if his gamble would pay off. But it did – and in spectacular fashion.

He began to worry that something was being kept from him – a certain edginess in the voices of officials, a certain reluctance to say at what stage the enquiry was. Then, on November 11 1963 the Volkstimme paper, official organ of the communist party of Austria, broke a sensational story about police inspector Karl Silberbauer pending an investigation into the arrest of Anne Frank and her family. It mooted the possibility of a war crimes trial. It seemed that Wiesenthal was not the only man on his tail; communists – a group that suffered heavily under the Third Reich – had also been pursuing the guilty man.

Wiesenthal believes that a communist sympathiser who also happened to be a member of the police force leaked the news of the Justice Ministry enquiry to some of his left wing colleagues, thus providing the communist paper with a scoop of quite staggering proportions.

Silberbauer became an instant recluse behind the curtains of his modest apartment home in Vienna, refusing to talk with the hordes of journalists who turned up to try

Above: ***Adolf Hitler became a religious deity for many Nazis. Yet the only gospel he preached was one of hatred and murder.***

WIESENTHAL WAS CERTAIN THAT HE WAS ON THE TRAIL OF THE MAN WHO HAD ARRESTED ANNE AND HER FAMILY

Left: ***Otto Frank, the father of Anne, who survived the Holocaust to find his little girl's diary.***

"WHY PICK ON ME AFTER ALL THESE YEARS?" SAID SILBERBAUER. "I HAVE BEEN RAILROADED. I ONLY DID MY DUTY"

to talk with him about that infamous appointment with destiny he had kept all those years ago. Wiesenthal gave his address later to a Dutch newspaperman who managed to get a few well chosen words from the suspect. He said: "Why pick on me after all these years? I have been railroaded. I only did my duty. We have just bought some new furniture on instalment – how on earth am I going to pay for it now?" That is what it had come down to for a former proud member of Hitler's super-race – paying the bills for hire purchase home fittings.

SELFISH FEELINGS

"Don't you feel sorry sometimes for what you did?" asked the journalist, hoping to elicit some human response other than self-preservation from the man. "Sure I feel sorry," replied Silberbauer, "and sometimes I feel downright humiliated. Every time I take a streetcar now I have to buy a ticket like everybody else. I can no longer get by on my police pass. I bought her little book last week to see if I am in it, but I am not. I suppose I was the first person ever to touch it, to see it. Maybe I should have picked it up off the floor. Maybe then no-one would ever have heard of me."

Silberbauer didn't even come close to the division one of Nazi war criminals. He was, in what the journalist Hannah Arendt summed up in Adolf Eichmann, the epitome of "the banality of evil". Wiesenthal was not particularly interested in what happened to Silberbauer – his success came from the fact that the man who had arrested Anne Frank had been found.

Wiesenthal learned that Silberbauer – in accordance with postwar dictates set by the victorious allied powers – had submitted to a de-Nazification tribunal before he could reclaim his pre-war police job. Enquiries from his superiors found he was not responsible for deporting the Franks and therefore not guilty of war crimes. He kept his job, his pension, his rights.

Yet Wiesenthal was able to go back to the pimply youths who became heady with the martial music and imagery of the Third Reich, and say to them that here was the man who confessed to arresting a real family with a real daughter who wrote a real book that shamed them and their kind. He had proved beyond any doubt that she had existed and, by extension, that the Holocaust that had snuffed out her young, unfulfilled life had also existed.

Silberbauer didn't matter a jot. But the establishment of the fact that he had walked through the door and arrested them mattered enormously when it came to fighting the propaganda of the new Nazis.

HE HAD PROVED BEYOND REASONABLE DOUBT – BEYOND ANY DOUBT – THAT ANNE FRANK HAD EXISTED

Right: ***Anne Frank's statue in Amsterdam, a memorial to a little girl whose courage equalled that of 10,000 men.***